Arthur Gregor
SELECTED POEMS

Books by Arthur Gregor

SELECTED POEMS (1971)
A BED BY THE SEA (1970)
FIGURE IN THE DOOR (1968)
BASIC MOVEMENTS (1966)
DECLENSIONS OF A REFRAIN (1957)
OCTAVIAN SHOOTING TARGETS (1954)

Arthur Gregor
SELECTED POEMS

Doubleday & Company, Inc.
Garden City, New York   1971

The author wishes to thank the editors and publishers of all of the following for their permission to reprint the poems in this and earlier collections. A number of the poems appear in this volume in slightly revised form. Dates of composition are given at the end of those poems for which the date seems significant.

The poems, A Tree Unlike Others, The Likeness, The Calm, Reply to a Friend in New England, Shadowplay, Irreconcilables, Gentle Lamb, Unalterables and Spirits, Dancing appeared originally in The New Yorker. The poems, Blackout, Ritual, The Mind Placed in a Room, Octavian Shooting Targets, A Mode of Hangings, Basic Movements, At Twenty or So (Twenty or So), Song Without Words, Enchanted Flowers, The Unworldliness that He Creates, Short Poem, The Statue, Sleep Took Me Far (Lack of Stand), Gift of the Firebird and Addressed to the Firebird appeared originally in Poetry, Copyright © 1947, 1949, 1951, 1956, 1958, 1960, 1965, 1966, 1967, 1969, 1971 by The Modern Poetry Association. Other poems originally appeared in Sewanee Review, The Nation, Prism, the Chicago Tribune (Today's Poets), New World Writing, Prairie Schooner, Poetry-London-New York and Yale Poetry Review, The Daughters of Jerusalem, Poem, Copyright 1947 by Yale Poetry Review, Quarterly Review of Literature, POEM II, Copyright 1951 by Theodore Russell Weiss, Quarterly Review of Literature, Estufa Fria, Autumn Mood, A Courtship, Lutenist, Alluding to . . . , Copyright © 1967, 1969 by Quarterly Review of Literature, Accent, Of Caligula, Bach and the Seascape, Copyright 1948 by Accent,

To Benjamin Goldenberg, my father,
and the memory of
    Regine Reiss Goldenberg, my mother.

CONTENTS

from FIGURE IN THE DOOR, 1968

SOME POEMS HITHERTO UNCOLLECTED

SOME NEW POEMS

Arthur Gregor
SELECTED POEMS

It is experience that must prove the existence of anything.

—Sri Atmananda

Was ist deine leidenste Erfahrung?
Ist dir Trinken bitter, werde Wein.

—Rainer Maria Rilke

from
OCTAVIAN
SHOOTING
TARGETS,
1954

BLACKOUT

When Europe and romanticism
coasted below resounding blackouts
like an airsick sofa, and Petrarch
sat weeping for wisdom's sake
and the unsung death of lemon bushes,
and Florence coughed out in blood
her ornate fountains of illustrious
merchants, I harbored, O My People,
I harbored mediterranean salons
for white fingers and Scarlatti.

Hitler was an expert at entertaining.
All the world said he was madder
than Caligula. Nevertheless he was
quicker than his own industrialists,
well disposed to great Danes,
and at evening from mountains
pointed out his panorama: smoke
and crematoria, the Simple Right
To Live all gone—and then
"Tara tara tara" on his forest horn.

The sensitive, the disillusioned
in America pantomimed a sad pavane:
Justice dead, the Pure all lost;
and scuttling coffins planted tiny islands
for purity to prosper. It was here
that I looked in, scouting on my life-
boat's murdered rubbish, and it was here
I faced angels on rococo instruments,

saw the grand staircase where
fantastic shepherds rose wet from
a ridiculous sea, memory   memory

1946

THE DAUGHTERS OF JERUSALEM

to Fred and Rhoda Goldenberg

The daughters of Jerusalem
carried water jugs and grapes;
outside the city they built
a fire; the rooftops were flat
and white. From across the desert
came white doves and the quartet
came from the palace. Darius, the
handsome Roman, strutted by
in his carnival uniform.
The daughters blushed; it was
before the temple fell.

What virtuoso, what agency
in Washington, in winter hotels
of India, what further slogans,
what further outrage, what
wedding night of lions in
lilac parks where emperors waltz,
will bring back such sabbath,
such easy ways of virgins
bearing water jugs, what
crematoria, what Ave Maria:
O Nations   Nations

The beach of Tel-Aviv is a fine
beach, umbrellas tilted, jazz
from cafes, oranges floating by
on barges where 300 yards

out in the sea the refugee ships,
the ships and daughters stand
illegal; and Rachel, Rachel, the
orphan, pale and sick from
the sea, waves an olive twig that
the waves rushing white against
the prow have brought her.

1946

POEM

to Hannelore Axmann

So many pigeons in Columbus
Circle in America; go, Tierra,
go! It is past the wars
and the nuns are waiting at
seaports, at the entrance to
the park. The fountains in the
Villa d'Este are the most
beautiful fountains in all

of Italy, was a statement in
a survey on Western Civili-
zation, and on the Piazza della
Signoria, Perseus is slaying
the Medusa to this day. When
I was 12, I said: patria
nostra olim provincia Romana
erat, and landed, riding on

seahorses of gold, on centuries
and Cellini, bumps in front of
the Doge's palace holding hands
with Beatrice. What an inter-
minable link, I thought, with
many orators and many merchants
and Punchinello, Punchinello,
the idiot of the circus, he

whom we have wronged too
much, Lisa's delight when she

was 4, he who sits on
churchsteps bleeding end-
less harps from his
nailed down fingers, O Tierra,
O witches in a reddening
forest, O whoever, whatever

recalls this all; like certain
young men who turn on an
elegant street, who go on
past cathedrals jittery as
swans and princes who have
missed their cue, who have no
other chance, and have no
other chance. So many dead,

so many murdered, Tierra, and
there was the singer in the
valley of oranges, and there
were the snows, the emerald
crowns on fishes in der Arls-
bergergrotte, and there was
the silence, and there were
the madonnas at noon . . .

1946

RITUAL

To Tiberius the aura of the hot basin,
of towels and oils had the whiteness of
flamingoes, and it was here he brought
a book of poems and a small revolver,
holding Hindu rivers in his eyes
and virgin bodies yielding to the Holy
Cleansing. Shortly after, his devotee,
a young male servant frantic with
love and shame phoned the police
who knew and therefore never came.

Tiberius meanwhile stood naked, con-
centric to four long mirrors and looked
at himself from four angles. He turned right
and what the mirror translated was
idiomatic of his boyhood, village days,
cornflower fields, of friendship, and of
books and white doves fluttering. He turned
left and saw himself as a barefooted god,
a tourist with a golden haired naïveté
of wisdom, among ceramic horses scattered on

the sands of ancient Rome. It was here
that he had forgotten everything, that he
had found Orpheus, the cries of charioteers,
art, in fact, symbolic of sorrow at a perfect
sunset. The looking glass in front revealed him
as most dexterous in "what life has to offer,"
showed him fingering feathers and medieval

instruments, showed his effluent brown eyes,
whereupon he remarked: "These are the tears
of unfortunate birds upholding rosaries

to monsters in their silver seas."
It was the fourth mirror, showing Tiberius
as then he was, that caused him to throw himself
upon the floor wailing that all this had never been
his wish, but that such was his heritage:
the way of Immortals to outrage crime with crime,
and that he was Tiberius H. the fifth,
rich and 28 and life was much too
short, and so he had tried. It was then
that he stepped into his bath, poems and

revolver on the floor. Twisting in the steam
Tiberius realized his servant's fear and
thought of him: drumbeats, a tropical sunset,
the claws of mild jaguars; and again felt himself as being one with primitives and drums,
aware of sacrificial rivers rising uproarious
through lotus thickets, gliding fanatically
through him. And then   then   the shot was heard.
Buddha and the oriental heavens had done
the virgins wrong, the rivers were bottomless,

they had lost so much and wept bitterly.
The young servant frantic with love and shame
drove a dagger through his throat. The fourth
mirror shot, stood impotent as crumpled cello-
phane: the simulated god of adolescence was
mortal after all and bled profusely. Poets

cried for their poems abused on bathroom floors,
and motors, and throngs of passers-by ignorant of
their potency waited as Tiberius, all dressed,
left the last palace step, out for a good time.

1947

POEM II

Also according to the
frescoes at San Lorenzo
there was once a for-
tress; there were three
kings who rode unto

the city on white mules
contemplating; there were
the beggars and the women
selling alpenflowers.

And when we came to
the valleys of the Tatra
where for centuries
the partisans had put up
tents and fires

we were aware of a
strong smell of hay and
the sounds of horses
galloping across the
meadows and all along

the roadside stood the
saints with a bunch of
cornflowers in the folded
arms and the songs and
the calls at nightfall.

The fog was heavy on
the waters when the
exiles came to the
harbor; there was a world

that was gone or for
better or worse was
going; they came with
the memory of mountains,

laurels, disk throwers
in the noon arena; they
had great feeling for
the few non-belligerent
outposts, the naked pillars
unsought by Aeolus;

they welcomed the
harbor, the other home-
less weeping waiting wet
at the pier.

And when I was a boy
we drove through
the forest with
horses and sleigh

and later when I wore
long trousers and the
warriors came towards me
with spears held at an angle

Surely this is no
confession, you have
seen my shield
by now too obstinate
turn murderer at
my bedside—
surely you have known . . .

Also the medallions of
the Medici were arrayed
in magnificent splendor
and the guilds of Florence
were openly grateful
for so benevolent a family

The foxes were steadily
kept on the grounds
and Catherine bore nobly
her crown throughout
the bloody times of France.

And when I see the dead
swarm about the islands
of fruit, the islands of
yellow fruit and there is

silence and an early fall
of oranges, and I recall
my world, the spears
flashing in the sun

and when I see the high
rocks and the white of
the foam of the sea and hear
tall monks and the marvelous
airs of Monteverdi   O world
O homeless   O fortress

1947

OF CALIGULA, BACH AND THE SEASCAPE

The sky and
the blue seascape
and the waves in
normal upsurge
shaped as the boats
in Hat-shepsut's time
by no mere coincidence

bearing the Queen's
gold and carpets
down the sometimes
quiet waters where
later Caligula said
to Neptune

I am the God

and scores drowned
complete with armor
and wine jugs

and the roaring of
the waters was deeper
than the idiot's laughter
blacker than cuttlefish
hit by spear

The sky and
the blue debris

in the blue-white foam
and the seascape blue
when it is calm
the waves and a white
convoy
swan for more
than mere convenience

is what we have
without question

The sky and
the seascape and
the swan out in the sea
not too far never too close
bearing theory, ideal,
the silver prince of peace

he who will not strip
to suntan beside us
will not ever

as the blue blue
seascape will never
rush   sh   sh
against our fingers

but who will ever in
the folds of wings of swans
exist
as a Bach Chorale exists

bravura
bravura
in us

The sky and
it is blue in the forum
of scattered salvages,
bone, horn, jade monkeys
that sailors kept,
the blue of soothsayers
and a sterile hand

Tiberius at Capri

we know of leopards and
the feasts of German guards

and the waves and
the swan or a white
basilica

a heritage
quite complicated
quite without question

The sky and
the blue seascape
and the horn, the searose,
the idiot's laughter,
the prince and
the chorale

the blue debris and
the very small clouds
purple when the coasts
where the lotus grows
turn to the sun

1948

THE MIND PLACED
IN A ROOM
to Sari Dienes

An Arab leading a horse stops
at the edge of a cliff, looks
across the desert and calls
the hills beyond the desert
the evening hills of Gibraltar.
With a mind that is not of
the desert but is of a village

with grapes, flat roofs, white
walls, what is around him is
around him but is not within
him; so that what is around him
is like a blue vicinity seen the
instant after a dream, and for him
what is around him is not.

The universe that is he is his
mind and his mind is a village
at noon, or a princess, beautiful
from towers descended in green
bathing to the chantings of a
pious chanteuse. The beats and
guitars and voices of girls he

hears is as the music between
the dream and the unknown reality,
between the waking and the not
waking from an impossible distance

heard; and realizing the lost
horseshoe in the sand, and for
an instant conscious of sand, but

not as sand but as a Hindu holy
river or deep blue Como about
him, yells out (what is within him
is not what is but has been
or perhaps what as a real image
never has been) and again yells out
and reaches for the flower in

the sand, the one dark flower,
and reaches for the corals like
emeralds he sees as upturned
reptiles as bouquets in the sand,
and with his lips reaches for the
fountain, the one last fountain, fresh,
deep green and buried in the sand.

1948

OCTAVIAN SHOOTING TARGETS

The top hat, French poodle, the electric heart
flaring up at minute intervals,
you needn't run and be alarmed at this—
it is all quite harmless now. He was a god
some years ago, a fashionable myth,
once or twice on the best-seller list, and now
we will have him here. Those who have seen
his picture in newsreel or magazine will
recognize Octavian, looking still like a
late renascence of an adolescent's faded
dream. Before he comes his seconds will
appear but will not fire shots into
the garden air; a team of village cowboys
they will be ready when Octavian shoots
to play for him Cole Porter on Austrian
flutes. You are amazed, you wonder why?
You thought he had the Bible read to him
in bed; listened to Bohemian madrigals sung
by innocents in Nebraskan stables; had corn-
roses put in his hair by dreamy devotees,
watching from hedges, sitting in trees.
You did not know of this, his daily fate:
he requests to shoot targets each morning
at eight: Octavian, gray-blond, not old,
not young, artist of considerable fame.

The papers do much for glamor; elaborate
on a violent death: statues of Egyptian
ancient kings were found to exhale poisonous

breath in the halls of a southern water-
villa. A handsome farmhand, trained because
he is sufficiently talented by a well-
known, aging playwright-sportsman, has won
the seaskiing trophy in Peru—the rest
is left to the fierce imagination of not
a starving few. How those who had
made it, Octavian for one, had tasted
bitterly in Nebraskan stormy wheat; what
it was that caused it, had long begun
and why; why others must kill themselves,
driven, desperate, afraid to try (the young
man who had put Octavian up before he
had come to fame was found dead on a
subway track at theater time); what it is
that must be given to get at such gain
and how it is done; how those who
had helped Octavian on, powerful com-
patriots too weak to want vengeance, had
made of him their Nebraskan hero, their
pioneer; how he had lessened their fear;
and now you ask: why is Octavian here?

London took him in but he was bored, Taos,
Portofino and the like were counts and
millionaires have art students to lunch
he touched on briefly; Athens, Florence and
the Villa Borghese he ignored; pursued the
darker shadings of his restless soul to
harbors and a Nepal caravan; came across
a circus, hunting kangaroos, met the aerial
dancer, thought well of a Gypsy chieftain's
wife: believed for days he had found

some life. Interested in the doings of
foreign hordes occupying a foreign country,
in principle anti-hordes but frankly given to
their brutal charm, he gained permit to
a palace built by an American for the benefit
of art, a sort of 20th-century monastery where
only approved artistic expatriates practice
daily rites. And there, catching himself
one night on a secret expedition to an
Arab sacred ritual of 30 chosen sons, he
laughed out, roared a whole night, a clown
among clowns, and was seen publicly once more
before he withdrew, before he was done,
throwing away his flowers riding in a gilded
hearse through the boulevards of busy Oran.

You will find others here. Those who sit
in attic rooms dressed as movie queens
waiting to be interviewed. Audiences with
kings, extraordinary swims, prize winning
models at a Florida review, spin around
the backwalls of needy, furnished minds,
a world where priests sweep dust in corners:
crash as symbols, our clues, out of their
horror-night. Clutching newsreports
to iron window-bars, they sometimes tell
of recollections, quick visions breaking
through their screams: figures at a bath,
David in the Square, girl at her clavier.
These are chanced on, a hand to the castout
like artworks found intact in a defeated
town; to one in his night a slender
youth appears, dark and tearful

as if it were childhood burned by sun.
Another minute and we will have Octavian,
brought by attendants to the practice room.
Before he comes his seconds will appear,
but will not fire shots into the garden
air; a team of village cowboys, they will
be ready when Octavian shoots to play
for him Cole Porter on Austrian flutes.

1951

from
DECLENSIONS
OF A REFRAIN,
1957

DECLENSIONS
OF A REFRAIN

Light is a quality
the senses
cannot behold

to Rajeshwar and Susheela Dayal

1.
More or less is a relative gesture,
as is gain or loss.
More or less, treacherous or bolder
was hardly the point or plan.
We turned violators only
when what had ever been done
to affirm what is noble and true
was made nothing or little of,
and of such serviceable breaches
that leave course to conformity
we have had more than enough,
did all that had to be done.
What have we not defied? State
and household rule, watched gladly
charred remnants, log and fabric
that once were yard and school
disintegrate and smolder,
watched the flame give out.

2.
In Bach I heard it, saw it
in Cézanne, I knew it
standing on the cliffs near Cannes.

What happened? Noise of some children,
the usual sunset, the foam
of the sea in my hair, a Hindu
blowing a horn, and women
rushing down to the base of rocks.
What happened to me nightly in dreams
was no ancient saga, no succession
of symbols, the feeling was clear.
In dreams but a will-less recorder,
I had heard the pursued crossing
a river and seen the pursuers
crashing their own lungs and lances
in the onrush of a forbidding
ocean. I was on the ground
but had known my body lifted.

3.
That what must be done, be done
matters and not the assignment
of value. What has always mattered
is the reign of a presence, in the
innermost sleep common to all—
representative men as its
shadow enrobed and anointed—
though places and races and legends
differ, and the method of attack
and the mode of delivery do not always
agree, and the clearing that had
to be done by Asiatics,
the French, Turks, or the Hun,
or by those great women and men
whose state to be overcome
was mostly a situation

within, spanning end and
beginning, did likewise differ.

4.

What can be said of greatness
but that, all levels transcended,
mental notations fail
where all expressions fade, and that
that presence does not begin—
out of where can it begin since nothing
is greater—but is reached. So in men
that were great as to what made them great.
And so in all men. An arm,
outstretched, pointing toward the sky,
across a land, across a sea,
men listen, respond, and vast
are the lines of the men that follow.
Animals gather, trees begin to
whisper, among clusters of corals
voices of bones surge to an echo:
and a total landscape, inner,
outer, begins to be transformed.

5.

In us that ancient cry has cried.
What have we not deficd?
Solomon, king, we too
a Song of Songs would sing!
David, goatherd, our lot
is the lot dreamers perferred.
We follow to the arena
where clansmen and triumphant
royalty have gathered.

What was it caused the upheaval,
boxes left in a hurry, the theater
empty? The outcome that altered
a nation's developed ideal?
O king   O king   O king
after assertion and bout
how to assume reign of
the presence in us, else triumph
turn vain, and victory loss?

6.

Not in time was the journey long
but in that it was continuous
as in a dream wherein the process
is complicated and each incident
though seemingly unrelated
aids the final resolution
the logic not in the individual
scene (often contrary
to all my grain though I
sponsored them   the pain
so strong and varied to speak of it
is outlandish here) but in that
the various outbreaks brought me
there, from dream to dream
to a first calm that overcame me
in that distant harbor, the sun
at dawn more enormous and barbarous
than when it set in the Arabian Sea.

7.

And not until I stood *there*, did I
for the first time know I *am* one

with what I had heard in Bach,
had seen in Cézanne, one with the command,
the flight, the fight, the search,
the knowledge clearest of all
below layers and layers
of personality and sleep,
in vaults of simple luxury.
They speak of such caves, merely
the entrances to deeper reaches,
where the light that fumes
is a quality the senses cannot behold:
for them men have lain at the feet
of sacred mountains, have dared
circumference, fiery cold and peaks:
for the caves that rest in them
and stir like a burning marvel.

1955

WHEN A BOAT DRAWS NEAR

When a boat draws near and friends are forced to part,
when a widening sea marks them where they are
and what they cannot do; when a yard burns
and silent children watching hold each other's hands;
when a man in battle driving another to
the ground recognizes all he has to know;
when dreams are mounted just as waking dawns
and loss opens on a sight that stirs:

it happens then they forget themselves as
particular men, involved, and small; then, what they
might later call a blanked out mind, a state
of more than blood-relatedness, of peace,
a tear to which they hear themselves respond with:
"We knew this, what we would find, and *is*,
must happen to all men"—happened to them then.

THE CHASE

In search through gardens, woods,
in sedan, on horse, or foot,
the bird, the goose, the hare,
the jewel in the fish,
the nymph that lingers where
moss and water at the blare
of trumpets, horns, like dreamy
musings disappear: the nymph,
the goose, the bird, the hare
are nothing but excuse
for chasing what is glorious
in all and everywhere.

From *that* to *this* and not
the process turned about.
Why else would hunters bleed
and the hunted sing aloud?

A MODE OF HANGINGS

To stop at the window of a shop
that is closed, to wait at the corner
for that someone to pass one, someone
with whom recognition is manifested
like a stab, there is something in this.

A world to enter, a fresh reflection of one's past in surroundings
quite unfamiliar, a mode of hangings
over doors and mirrors that is common
but yet for the first time encountered.

The strangeness of strangers is canceled out
by the strangeness around them.
The will that brought them together
knows this and yearns for it,
to meet quite another in union.

And what is it occurs when strangers
lose their strangeness in the strangeness
around them until there is not even that,
and the will that brought them together
is achieved and merged?

Say that the hangings tremble. A presence
voids the surroundings. Say that it glides
from the figure of one to that of the other.
To wait at the corner for that someone
to pass one, there is something in this.

THE WINGBEAT

The bird. The bird moving. Wings beating against
the body, beating outward toward the building,
beating upward for the sake of mere survival:
a pigeon flying against the grayness of the day.
I have been witness to the bird coming past
my room in many a year, I in an ordinary pose,
busy or not, my sight by chance gripped by
the wingbeat against the window. I came to in
a public place, a theater or waiting room, when
I listened to some people talk. I knew at last,
though nothing at all was seen, what held them
was the caustic shadow, a thin, a darkened air.

The fluttering of wings of pigeons has meant
apprehension in the face of troubled kings,
has meant dryness at the time of harvest,
the madness of a tyrant in cases more extreme.
(The shadow came once in disguise into a palace room
rolling in its hands the allness and the whiteness
of the moon. A Ceasar, it might have been Caligula,
done with inadequate blood, tore at his mind
while boys and women leapt from windows naked
into tho flood). The fluttering has affected
different kings in different ways but
has always meant that darkness is upon a country,
that a falsehood is regarded as reality,
that the heart has lost its link to light—
its *other* sense that must behold and hold
what the bodily senses cannot sense or see.

About to be trapped by the descending blackness
as if it were a flag draped across housefronts,
a plague, a curtain let loose and coming down,
I remembered something. I was pulled to listen.
Something sang. I thought it sang to me. The fact is
it sings of itself, for no one in particular, for all.
Just then its song broke through to me, or I to it.
Always with me, so close it had escaped me,
my misery was I had missed, mistaken it
as it flew past my window, as it beat
its wings against the body, outward, upward
toward the sky. So the darkness broke. Nor was
what gleamed behind mere light, but more as if
in the crack of a curtain slit open by design
the outline of an angel shone, looking down,
a celestial framework, rocklike and benign.

Fluttering in me now as light, as sheerest joy
whose are the wings said to have left darkness in
my room? What is gone? Since not the shadow,
not the wingbeat, but that wherein these grow,
wherein they mount and fade beyond the evidence
of trail or scent, lives on: this more-than fullness
that turns my sight from form to formless,
from so-called bird to sea whose endlessness
culminates within, whose glare few have withstood,
and those who have, predict it is the fire
that will one day free the eyes of all.
Meanwhile, a rushing mob has overrun
the streets. "The bird! The bird!" they shout.

POEM

Venice at night and I
like the wakeful dreamer
or the dreaming walker,
like the hooded watchman
counting time, awake
and wakened by my cry.

A moment full, and rare
of course, moon in the canal
and moon cutting the statue
of a Doge on his horse,
only the ruler's head
and horse's mane were lit.

Stone bench, stone railing,
a former promenade
where I stood and sensed a
stillness still beyond my cry,
beyond boats sailing
to a brightness lived fully

only in a dream. Such was
the scene, these were the
constituents: artwork, water,
space and inner world;
several ways merging to a
single trend, and beyond.

Venice one with water,
leader one with horse,

I one with sound and sight,
one with that surging force
that flowed from ocean,
hero and his horse; and then

from sidecanals felt I
the inhabitants of ages come
as if looking and careful not
to be caught, and looking
their look aimed at distance
rose to a cry, a cry

in me. Compound of point
beyond, absolute, and
fogridden door and stairs from
dim waterways, the beauty
of a horse, and a Doge
certain of what he must say.

from
BASIC
MOVEMENTS,
1966

"In the world, not of it . . ."

BASIC MOVEMENTS

1.

He moves out of the dark
unto an empty place
a steersman if you like
at the helm in a fog
and what his mind contains
is more likely than not
at odds with rules of the night
and with a ship's log.

He steps with caution
as though a dancer on
an empty stage in sleep
moving in slow motion
his vision not heeded
ignored by the night
a heavy air settled on
city streets and ocean.

2.

He has moved out of the dark
has stepped forth
has lifted up one arm
the other held stretched out

He has opened his mouth
and not a sound
not a ripple
not a whishing in the air

audible, noticeable, anywhere . . .

3.

Therefore must love abound
love arrived at when
good attempts have failed,
brave steerings toward
important ends
have been inadequate.
How shall love be traced?
overhung by haze
nothing as its base . . .

AT TWENTY OR SO

There is nothing will define this look.
How I came to know of it I cannot know
but was more intimate with it, at twenty or so,
than with matters part of my existence then,
and in a clouded distance damp with dreams
saw it, heard it in wild imaginings
along an empty street, a river bank,
or reaching out, face downward, over a brook.

At twenty or so, I was so sure of it
only a lack of testing could have made
this so, and tried in ways I was convinced
I had to take to shape it near my breath,
locked in its look, to force the death
of the ignorance about the thing
I knew so well, for in a visual sense
I was ignorant of its high countenance.

And loved this look that would drive through me as
the first light barely perceptible in a path
between trees, the lightest touch of blossoms
on the faces of travelers still half asleep.
And loving that which would annihilate me so,
it has loved me well, and taught me since:
not confined to a stare or single phrase,
the object and the source of praise,
it is not captured in the eyes it floods.

SPIRITS, DANCING

Having put yourself on the way,
it is inevitable that you
should reach here. If in
your thoughts you've had
the notion of reward
as you fought to come this far,
banish them. And,
as penalty for entering,
shed the attitudes of worldly men
regarding us and this
celestial sphere where now
your spirit begs to enter.

From the extremity
to which you've come, you see
us sway as in a dance.
It is no sign that we
are happy. To be happy
is being a step removed
from happiness. Which we
never are. Nor are we sad.
Sorrow is man in the world,
and we, the total expression
and awareness of his state,
are sorrowful.

What seems to you,
who were taught to feel
we must fulfill

where the world has failed,
must turn to good the bad,
must invoke permanence
for material whose law
and will it is to die—
what seems to you, driven here
by urgency, a dance
is nothing but the pain in the world
which we like a mirror contain.

To sway is to depart
as branches from a stem,
as shadows from foliage
thick and dark—
and to depart is what is pain.
What you must know before
you enter this domain
and learn the ways of which
we shall not speak is this
first truth of what you are:
a sorrow, a sorrow
begging for home. Or you
would not have come this far.

A SINGLE FLOWER
OF THE FIELD

A single flower of the field—
one in a great multitude—
not singled out by gatherers
or those who like to speak
of that which is unique,
said to the wind about to tear
it at its root: "Do what you will!

"Your force across this field
stings every vein in me.
Dumbstruck I was when first
you took my pollen and my leaves.
But you have seen yourself in me,
have made me what you are,
and my oblivion has ceased."

ST. FRANCIS

All along its course
there is nothing a river excludes
once part of its flow.
Driftwood, leaves, a flower
tossed from shore, all make
a common journey. Preferred
passage exists for none
and at the end, when the river
joins a larger force—
a larger inland water or the sea—
there is absolutely nothing
the broader body does not absorb.

He of Assisi was such a river,
a form through which the stream
could work its will.
And when he beheld the doves aflutter
and saw not feathers but
the purest movement in their wings,
not air but a denseness of lilacs
by which the movement was sustained,
he called the birds unto himself,
accepted them
and told them who they were.

And he, the river, brought them to the point
where all that flows
flows on into a city of
fantastic light. There the birds
could see their songs

as solid frameworks in the sky.
He told them so, and they
knew then that this was so
and trembled before him
who had become for them the stream
and beyond the river's end the source
toward which their own wing-movement flows.

ASSISI AND ENVIRONS

The earth more than the relics
and the timely man-made things—
the land's variety richly
developed, valleys and hills,
cedar lanes and olive groves,
a fertile green differing in tone,
the gentle roads and streams—
the scene unified and yielding like a plant
laden with fruit—painters of long ago
have shown this country so—
arches, water-spans and buildings all
in the same irregular local stone:
the earth more than most other things
suggests now who it was
who once walked over it.

Between the leaves on trees, above
the field where a peasant stacks up hay
while his horses graze nearby
and other fully laden carts
are chased by barking dogs,
between the sight of one such scene
and of another, and between
the bells, the many bells,
the sounds of cymbals hang,
of trumpets and of all such instruments
suitable for the processional,
the timid, unobtrusive passing of
the soul in whom the very soil
reflects itself, becomes itself
as the child coming to life in air.

That such have passed here,
have scattered from their sleeve
of coarsest cloth a wind
of jasmine scent, have reigned
as evidence of what is possible
in man, have dispelled the notion
where they dwelled that man's life
is identical with
the nature of the earth,
have subdued this ignorance
the way an Eastern saint laid low
the deadliest of snakes
by doing no more than lifting up
his hand and walking lightly by
as days go by, and all of time.

To that, to that expression of
the height in man that swept
across these parts as a star
descends across the sky,
to that this land does testify.
Those who seek through living
evidence to understand can catch
between the sounds they hear
the land's perpetual chant
and see beneath the surfaces of trees,
of fields and hills as if beneath a sea
that look of timelessness, of love
in the eyes of those accomplished ones
who walked here once and now still hold
deep in their faces this land, as of old.

A TREE UNLIKE OTHERS

There is a tree by the lake
bending way out over the water,
straining over the surface,
like a forlorn wanderer
looking down from a bridge
while most of a city sleeps.

Something so aloof, almost lost
about that tree stubbornly
turning away from others,
patiently straining to see
what others along the shore
cannot catch, like those of us who,
unwilling to linger,
go past and see only
the changes that most of us see.

But the tree has left nothing
behind. Straining over the water,
what does it catch
with endurance and calm
but the image of trees?
And what does it see
beneath the sky in the lake
but leaves and birds on a tree's
bent form, and the leaves
and the birds on each arm
that every season
have come and have gone?

LETTER FROM MEXICO

1.

Everything I see, have absorbed, and am
is my letter to you whose gentle countenance
shines behind the streams I cross, the scenes
I look at from trains or at sunset from
my window at a hotel. Even the rug
for sale at a Sunday market
has something to do with you
as I think of it in front of my fireplace
in my room. And when at night the body seeks
some shimmering shade, some lyrical suggestion
of its dark, its sorrowheavy avenue,
it is of you I sing, whom I
can hardly name, whose smile is like the cast
of something permanent, a work of maddening faith
as that of a dead young girl afloat
in a quiet river, stagnant lake
and seen in the mind or in a dream.

My life, my innermost self held back
the way the clarity in light and seas,
the steady hum of women's voices out of which
haunting songs are spun, keep themselves
held back in fabulous caves; my stepping forth
in the world unknowingly, like everyone
a child in darkness; my trips in which
towns and faces, seas and landscape come,
depart as in a dream; my struggle to
attune myself within the law to be as love,
to stand, view, absorb, to love as love:

each action an attempt to flow toward you
and speak the way a wind across vast plains
around the edges of fragile plants communicates.

2.

Here in Mexico I think of you in Pennsylvania.
A walk one afternoon upward in a brook,
the fresh but still pale green of early spring,
the young leaves slightly shimmering
in the barely clouded sky reflected in
the shallow stream, the slate along one side
formed into a straight, a sculptured line.
You did not think at first that nature
could have meant it so: a scene as Cézanne
might have painted it. How could we express
what we both knew? It was the scene
contained the most in us. Therein we flowed.
Therein, and closer than hand to hand,
one by recognition that we are, could come
to the brink beyond which separation is
no more. As waves fall back upon a common sea,
could achieve the common substance that we are.
We knew the scene was all. Love itself its own
expression. Nothing needed but to yield.
As sounds submitting to a voice within
are formed into a perfect song, by dying to
the scene could stamp out every thought,
each limiting demand with proud contempt!

3.

You, you who are gentle, who sense the choir of the soul
that shines upon the world through eyes
like those of animals in a paradisaic pose:

you are not just an image to my mind.
The varied views of an enchanted night
flare up around a candle in an open room.
You are the wanderer with inward eye
whose footprints are the only ones
in shallows of an ancient, moonlit coast.
You are the student about to follow
a traditional request. You walk along the road
that takes you to the dwelling place of ancestors.
You hear the call of birds in palms.
Toward where you go your welcome is immense.
How do we contain such goodness in a scene?
You are the voice of girls sequestered in a grove
declaring love to him who dwells within each heart,
listening among the leaves, their ears over streams,
praying they may learn his nearness from his flute.

You are the meaning of the truly human sense.
What is a jasmine spray, a lily without scent?
Secretly, behind their thoughts, you are
the lyrical significance of those
who would be rather human than machine.
You are all that I am certain of,
are that which in the gesture of a hand, a
quickly passing look, I catch a glimpse of.

4.
The world threatens you. What is a candle in a darkness
when that darkness is a flood of artificial lights?
An age like an avenue needs narrow gaps for those
qualified to make their way to a hill of light
for the comfort in the sleep of all.
And you, your heart so young, so capable, wait

to receive awakening stemming from your own kind.
But this grossly transgressed world would assume
an echo needs no voice behind it,
a room no smile, a song no star in the throat.

Because of this I cherish you the more,
would vanish at each moment for your need.
The age does nothing to instruct us
to turn our faces toward a perfect union
entwined with each transforming moment
in a Pennsylvania scene. It is for you
I seek some knowledge in the hidden laws
that chart an order. Like a music in the night
attempt a poem to the wind.
Were chaos all, wherefrom the gentleness
that strikes the hardest where you walk,
shames those who throw at it their guilt?

5.
Thoughts that come up at the light of a candle
are phrases for lines, the beginning of a letter to you,
of a kind I am not qualified to formulate.
Who but the saints and sages who seldom write
are competent as scribes? To contain
the single essence in a word, a sacred syllable,
to lift the gauze from a scene of watered beauty,
fill a void with a look so firm
so much itself it is the very core of love:
transmit to ready souls the way insects and wind
transfer the ripened seed from open buds
to furrowed soil. Such the events in consciousness
inscribed upon the parchment that my being is.

6.

Imagine a dark night. A man on a lake all by himself
in a boat that can contain him only. All at once
he sees light streaming forth from the water
below him, light concentrated in a spot near him,
a radiance behind deaths and deaths of seas,
a brilliance of topaz flaming, and also from below,
the sweetness, the incomprehensible sweetness
of watervoices singing, spinning a melody at play.
He flees the scene. He is becoming one
of not this world nor is he as yet
of another. He rows, his haste a mixture of
joy and bewilderment that is the agony of those
who are blessed and are hunted by heaven,
for a while finds refuge in the empty halls
of an ancient castle. The tears he will shed
unable to tear the music from his soul,
the weakened habit that still holds him,
forces him to cling to the by now
deserted habitation; his cry to be near again
to the sweetness he once encountered:
these the events, the conflicts in the phrases
of the letter he is living from then on.
Not yet the expression of the primal glory,
nor any longer an example of addiction to a world
whose fabric has been shown him
as the background of only illusion,
he is a message, his person a poem, a letter,
his charge not to accost like the Ancient Mariner
but gently to impart the truth of his fantastic tale
to others, strangers in this world, like you.

7.

Could I but give voice to the depth that determines
the ardor in visible objects, imparts
those incomprehensible shadings in the sounds
of harps—or in these parts guitars—
that return to nestle deep within one's being
as gems, as flowers the eye cannot behold
cling to the walls of underwater caverns,
as lilies nestle in the nostrils of those
lowered in the ground. Could I with such voice
address you, you, my deepest meaning!
Could I find my stand in the essence of love
from where everything must surely be seen
as nothing but creative play! Could I thus rid
myself of falsehoods, for every endeavor is false,
an evasion, compared to the longing that leads
to the stand where all that lives is seen
as love, and love the only life that is.

That I might then perhaps begin to tell you
of a Mexican market, men and women kneeling
at the open gate to the church in the center,
the altar hung with gauze of purest blue,
thick clouds of incense rising, and then at the end
of service, the sonorous depth of a Bach toccata
played well on an organ in this town of mostly peasants.
Might then start to fathom something of the totality,
the inexhaustible beauty in this scene,
and thus let an adequate message begin,
the first correct phrases of not a letter so much
as a dictate, that I might then take down.

San Miguel, 1960

ONE WINTRY DAY
SUNNY AND CLEAR

One wintry day sunny and clear
I came quite unexpectedly
upon a very small stream below
the road where I had walked.
It is impossible to say
there is a thing bright as
the brightness that day
which only the haze that burns
when a thing is recognized
and just as
its outlines disappear,
or perhaps the dissolution of
a bad fate in a dream
can approximate.

I stopped a while to lean over
the bridge—not exactly that
but a tiniest span that led
across the stream.
I looked below. Water turned
heavily, was wintry, was dark.
I looked around. Snow covered
the fields on either side.
It came, the little stream,
I could not tell from where
behind a bend and faded out
I could not follow it to
its end out in
the vast white field.

It was morning, I had not been
up for long and now recalled
a dream: with arms stretched out
I had thrown myself
had thrown myself
with arms held wide apart
upon the ground. In the dream
a happiness had then come over me
enveloped me like air
like clear edges of a sea
spreading far out to enfold
long reaches of a sound
I am the earth
I am the sky

A SUNBATHER
IN LATE OCTOBER

On the bank of the river
covered by a haze as if
there hung a bird—
its head deep in the sky,
its wings so immense
they are always there—
a young sunbather lay
in the dry grass reclined
as on a bed
waiting to submit
to the power of
the autumn sun whose rays
could scarcely penetrate
the veils of thick white air.

From time to time
behind the haze
a ship appeared
whose bulk looked vague
in the diffusing
manner of the day.
No one could say
if men hung in its masts
dead or alive
intent on
spotting the bird
kept out of sight
by the pervasive glare.

In such anticipation
the young sunbather lay
his legs apart
like a woman, enraptured by
the whir of wings,
waiting for mysterious heat
to sting his bones,
for haze to wipe his body out,
for unexpected magic in the air
like a bird with giant beak
to pick his flesh,
eager to recognize his disembodied self
in the mirror blazing in the air!
Why else was he there?

SONG WITHOUT WORDS

It does not depend on music for its composition.
Music sometimes transcribes it. Words
contribute toward it if meant to return
to the source from where they emerged and continue
this moment to flow; articulation
that often follows once a thing
has been transcended by knowing it
dissolved in experience by means of experience:
so rain falls having been transformed
by means of some earthly act in the realm
of constant transformation into
its own essence where it is all things,
all things in heaven, and there transformed
to return with the freshness, the blessing
it has gathered in its constant cycle,
to settle on a pond, a leaf,
on the hand of someone awakened from dream.
What does it tell, the song in the twilight moment?
What it tells is not gathered, nor lifts and curls
about the edge of a town, a forest,
or any brightening scene, is not a fog
or a dew drawing back and upward at the commanded
hour, though that its meaning is also evaporation,
a line forever receding, forever eluding
the eye's limit, beyond the capture of sound,
it would seem. What it tells is not grasped
in a way indistinguishable from the method
or style that conveys it. What it tells is not
mere composition conducive to study,
not that a leaf is carried in a wind,

nor that a fall of rain has brought
a musician back from his dream, not that
a bird walking on water opened its wings
at the sound of wind brushing the pond's surface,
nor that a dreamer lies dying of infinite sorrow
while the wind does not shut the door to awake him
nor opens it wide enough for the light
to steam in; nor even tells in specific terms
though something of that impression surely remains:
that the line between heaven and earth
is supremely fixed—though deceitfully thin
for the heart that is frail, the ear
that listens for sounds beyond their natural place,
the eye that mistakes the instant after
experience when the world is blurred and
transformed to a song no one hears, for a tear.

RUNAWAY SPIRIT

At night when the streets were still
and most people in the city
had slipped deep into sleep,
a whisper ran down pavements,
air curling like a tornado
whizzing up and down like
a siren or some whistling freak,
a wailing clinging to shut doors,
to windows without life in them.
And this is what it was:
air whining to be earth,
spirit howling for body and face.

And this is what it said,
the freakish thing of air,
the impulse up and down the street
as if it wished to raid
the earth: "Without legs, arms,
without face in the mirror,
without means to attempt
to experience what I am,
without human attributes
what abstract thing am I!
As a tree feels itself most
when a storm tears at its roots,

as lovers who cannot escape the fact
that forms of love must end
love their love best
when they part; as a traveler

seeing an old town on a hill,
bright roofs and towers like a crown
speeding away from him
feels first what he has lost:
what lives knows itself best
when it is suffering most.
It may be odd of me
to demand again the earth,

who know so well its pain,
but when a city sleeps
and I perceive and feel
what is in people's dreams
no matter what they dream,
I turn into a runaway spirit
willing to give all I can
for life in the flesh again."
And so it wailed and whirred,
and all across the city in
the hours between twelve and dawn
this yearning was abroad.

ODE TO THE STRANGER

1.

Seeing you come out of the darkness
the empty street presenting you to the night,
you absolutely wiped me out—
my eyes, the trembling of my hands,
all of my presence in the night
wiped out by the unfolding of
your face, your body and face.

Is it possible that out of the darkness
out of the emptiness of the street
out of the motion water imparts to air
you rose in the night, walked
as surely only a god can give all
of himself to the three dimensions,
scattering before and after him

the reverence and hush that attend
an event fulfilled like a ritual.
And with it I went, with your rising,
your walking past and away, went as
the air you displaced and the space
you filled, at each step the air you
displaced and the space you filled.

2.

Although I did not know who you were
as I intermingled with
the changes you caused in the air,

quick sights of conditions
such as appear in flashes—
sudden views at the end of thoughts

of which hardly a glimmer remains
to remember—revealed you.
These flared up in me as though I

were the screen of your being,
the background where the truth of what you are
is acted out not only by

spirits eluding discernment
but by a chorus in a tragedy
intoning what cannot be avoided.

3.
     i
Cause for the wave
to lift itself
and strive for the height
needed to recede.

A wave is restless in
the heaviness of the sea.
A rule like a dumb thing
that asks not but acts

as ordered, makes a wave
seek to spread out in air,
a flower giving a rain
of petals to the wind.

Is a wave ever as much
a wave as when it is
an invisible film on
your face, when your fingers

touching your skin
are astonished by the spray,
and the best of messages
drifts into your dream?

ii
Cause also not only for hopes
of others to find themselves
in accordance with their needs
but   O bitter paradox
main figure as well in
the drama of anguish and fear.

I see a firing squad,
you, a young sailor
tied at your wrists.
Churchbells are raging as if
all of the wind of the sea
had swept into steeples.

I see an entire city kneeling,
a girl throwing open a window
tossing you a rose.
The bullets, and you are swaying
as though tied to a mast
at sea in the wildest storm.

I see you centuries earlier
blind and cast out,
a young girl, your staff,
taking you off
to dwell among beggars:
you, a prince in this world.

4.
Prince   Prince
failed symbol because
those who once were poor
and lived in fields
had to deride you
since they could not forget
the splendor on mountain tops,

the light behind windows
when they stole to the grounds
for lutes in the air,
songs whose melancholy key
they understood.

How could they forget you?
How fail to want to emulate you?

You, who opened the glass door.
You, who accumulate the sights
and distances sung in psalms—

you, who sat on your horse
the sun streaming from your cloth . . .

Prince   Prince nevertheless
when in this age
as stranger you rise

and the street is silent

and the light you scatter
you cannot see

5.
    i
Behind the floral growth
of frost on glass
is a wind

Behind the traditional hum
putting a child asleep
is a nod

and a word

and from the word
the beat and phrases
forming in an empty street

    ii
Of all that lives in you
you do not comprehend
start nor end

only the moment when
you stride in full bloom
down the pavement

gives acknowledgment.
As if you could feel
the spaces you fill

as if a fragrance
you cannot trace to the source
flooded each sense.

6.
When out of the darkness you rose
and my hands, my eyes,
my presence attending the night
flowed into your face,
your body and face,
what was I, am I,
but what you are!

You, without whom the quest
for towers once sanctified,
for walls in the first morning light,
for vistas afloat
in wells of caverns
aglow again in your eyes,
could not be: you

who strive always to strive.
Ultimately, the turns you take
as you pass on again
into the dark, are part
of the way, not delay.
Who, who is there can match
your nobility! The extent of which,

the hails and blares acclaiming it,
you cannot know: you, who receive
no more than hints or glimmers
in the morning of your day—
in the day when you and no other
are the same! Even this night
did not reveal your name.

from
FIGURE
IN THE DOOR,
1968

THE LIKENESS

How can you live, how exist
without assurance of
or at least the memory of
someone, something
fantastic, marvelous
always behind you,
a hand, grip on your shoulder,
a presence surrounding you
as a shell surrounds what lives inside?
Song closer to you than flutter to wing!
Words more antique than age!

Without it—call it intimacy,
your intimate connection—
how do you stand vis-à-vis
the multiplicity of things,
a tree, fence, grass, person in your path?
Unless you find in them
that quality no one defines,
how do you love, what do you
whisper, what song
do you share in the dark?

Without it I am as someone
lost from his caravan
a sandstorm whipping him;
someone out to find help on a frozen sea,
man alone on a waste of ice
imagining as the vast and hazy
emptiness absorbs him

a tattered though victorious
humanity coming toward him,
soldiers linking arms,
a populace with banners
singing and beating drums.

Without it
I am cut off.
I await its sound.
I ravage memory
for sight of it, its melody.
I shape with bare
and desperate hands
its likeness in myself.

THE CALM

1.
Attempt at all times closeness to
the conflict you are in.
Not so as to dwell upon
dulling details of the cause
but to be aware of this:
that you are always in between
a white-clad calm that
at long intervals comes down

and the steady turmoil at the base:
a sea seething,
a field devastated,
a man weeping, stone and dust
turned human for as long as
being human can be endured.

2.

Closeness to the conflict is
your nearness to its source.
The more fully a singer sings of
the pure anguish of your state,
the deeper the thought in you
that you too are being heard.
The turmoil in the water is often in
the surface that is thin.
When you cry because where you had been
the coast was calm, your small boat
in the sand left upside down,
the white-clad figure moving toward you
spanning sea and sun,
bemoan, bemoan it is no longer so!
The calm that will come again
                  was long ago!

WHAT IS HUMAN IN ME

What is human in me—
dreams that repeat,
incitement of figures
riding in on waves—
sorrow in me
that what arises
must in like manner fade—
face bent over my sleep
easing the pain when I woke—
what is meaningful to me
must from time to time at least
be my reality,
not unlike the soil
a plant needs to grow
must be around me—
faces in whom
is deeply inscribed
feeling for suffering,
eyes that state
facts that can't be said.
No one can take bloom in hands,
though it may seep through pores
and make one shudder in the dark.
Walls I seek
with flowers strung from top,
the height where hidden gardens start,
full life of the senses, of the heart,
floats I can imagine but not see—
the invisible suggested by
the visible to stir
what is human in me.

REPLY TO A FRIEND
IN NEW ENGLAND

I have your note.
Sorry to read you're lonely.
You have not found the joy you went for.
I know the bay you're visiting.
There the visual things
suggest the condition you feel,
flap in one's soul
like laundry hung to dry.
The sky is static there,
thin clouds the color of
swans' wings let through
a light that reaches corners
but has not the power
to illuminate.

Water beats against the stones
below the strip where people sit,
the boats out in the bay
look as though they give themselves
to being tossed about,
and not much happens.
The shadow of a bird
(wings spread fully out
the bird seems not to move,
seems painted on the air)
hovers over the reflection in
the water of a boat,
gray spreading over gray.
Shadows in this bay

that seek each other out,
cannot be kept apart,
nor does one blank the other out
escaping thus the separateness
that all decry, the flow
and sway of each with which
each must identify.
Is this then the law
that all must learn to live
who visit where you are
or any other strip of coast:
identity must be retained?
loneliness is part
of being self-contained?

In this bay where you have come,
where the coast is defined
by what you see—
by monotone and static sky—
you like others must confront:
the limited return
of what you want.
All day long the light is faint.
The repeated view of sails,
taken for white flags
implying hope, is bleak.
You have not found another way,
no other way but inward for
the self-assuring joy you seek.

SHADOWPLAY

Dead to the world, I was cast back
to move again among familiar shapes.
The state where I had been
cannot be described. There were
no objects there, but in
full strength and in pure form
the presence that takes speech
and mind away when feelings
are stirred by a person's momentary stay
pale as early evening in the door.

I knew when I was back it was
not nothingness had held me there.
That part in me which bears
no semblance to my body's line
on paper or in falling light
was then about to be received
like a cloth brought to be laid
across arms wide as space,
by a love gentler than air
and voices, voices behind clouds.

Not yet allowed, some forces dark
and fleeting came and drew me back—
from high walks where structures hold
all time and things that pass—
back to shadows that glide across
the shadow of my hands,
back to the movement of clouds,
the light at dark, the noted hush,

the moment of the figure in the door,
back to my repeated effort among
the things where I have walked before.

ESTUFA FRIA*

1.
Clouds the shape of
chalk tracings of wings
above the city by the sea.
The shutters closed at noon.
A wave rippling far out.
A murmur running down
an empty street.
Around the winged statue in
the port people sit,
cars are parked.

The hand of the giant clock
has turned one slot
to the sound of bells.

Movement starts.
Wave and wing begin to pale.

———————

* A tropical garden in Lisbon

An air drifts by
as if from foreign parts.

In an area set aside
for music, birds and solitude,
book-in-hand a figure walks.

2.
Dissolve, body, forget
the melancholy of
solitary steps.
Be leaf of palm,
be glitter of small birds.
Be tiny pool,
the glidings of
the single swan.
Music pours from
all sides, a silence
from the wings above.
And what the book contains
is nothing but the spelling of

one word
one word . . .

3.
. . . body of love

even the faded figures
in ruined frescoes,
in restored rooms

the portraits of famous masters
fix their eyes on you

the singer's hand
points at you

cloud wings and murmurs
hang about your head,
a diffuse succession
from the sky

and far above the historic plains,
the mountains far away—
whirls of snow
like a dreamer's gestures in the air—
lift up and stream to you

body of love
by the sea.

THE LOVE-FANATIC

The dilemma of wanting not just
to taste but to possess
glorious, impossible love
can be described as this:
I have dared alone in my boat
far out beyond where any sea-
searching fanatic should.
I find the shape I want to hold.
We burn in a burning haze.
Incited by this fire
and again seeking out the spot
the shape on water cannot be found.
Though spirit hungers, I share
the urge of hound for hound.
I hear in the winds nothing but
chords from lost love's lyre
and a turbulent bloodstream
makes me seek far and farther out.

No flares or warning signals
are sent aloft from shore.
Indifferent to my spirit's needs
life goes on there as before.
True, special gardens are there
for healing, serene and secure,
but it is not serenity I've dared
far out for, but love
for which there is no cure.
For which I've set sail again
seeing in my mind a priest

with crucifix above the sea
to pacify the storm or bless
the drowned who had to learn that:
the vision on the water—
not merely an angelic creature
but fiery, perfect flesh and blood—
is a reality
they could not keep, but found.

SEPTEMBER SONG

A cool evening in early fall.
The evening brisk yet frail
thin as a river's skin
like a canvas of air open to tracings:
people, shops, traffic lights and cars
briefly imprinted on the evening's surface—
a painter's strokes on a watery base.

On the radio a rarely performed
Schubert work. Vienna a long time ago.
I walked there once . . . ah, much more
than once. A statue in
a basin in a square dedicated to
the penniless, the dreamridden
genius, Schubertplatz, Schubert-
gasse, Schubertallee—

a damp evening, the streets
lit dimly by electric bulbs
in streetlamps where not long ago
gas had flickered,
the whole flickering evening drifting by
in the darkness under the bridges
of the Danube canal.

Adagio. The width, the height,
the length of the evening spread,
have far-reaching effects
like a crack in a glass,

the brush of time on a sensitive brow,
a pebble on a surface that cannot endure.

Adagio. The slowness, transitions
from hardly discernible shadings
to deepening frown, the pain
that comes with the changes in music,
creeps into one's being like the breath
from gratings in streets
when the temperature has fallen to zero,

these have not the power now
to rouse a question.
The question is gone.
Gone also the youthful agitation
that there is one.

In supreme naturalness
fades the statue of Schubert's
nineteenth-century head.

In supreme naturalness
the shifts and fadings
of a brief walk one brief evening
one brief evening one brief fall.

DON CARLOS,
SATURDAY AFTERNOON

Alone! Who does not know the meaning of
alone? Granted, there is a world outside,
houses and streets are wet,
people run in and out of cars.
In the story sung on the air
each character is in the end alone.
A Spanish prince still loves the woman
who has become his father's bride.
A conquering Court attends the saving
of fallen Christians at the stake.
Although one hears a lofty gloria,
the prince in prison chains cries out,
betrayed, he thinks, by the one he loved
and by the friend in whom he believed.

Does it really help that being alone
is one condition shared by all?
The drama off-stage is no less complex.
Although one may assume that
disparate parts that do not always lock
in place are woven by a common thread,
the burden is not lessened for all that.
Not lessened by bewildered heads
and muffled cries, nor by the fact
that the sky's been agitated all day long,
that men in raincoats stumble across
slippery roofs, and that the very air
is dense with wriggling bacteria
which show up under a powerful glass.

AUTUMN MOOD

The smell that flames impart to air
of a fire tended and controlled
in a garden or clearing in
an autumn wood

stirs the recumbent fellow in
the body's inner room
where not a hallway leads,
no easy turn of knob can reach.

Pensive and full
of weeping thoughts he lies,
to a violent strength aroused
when invading smells and sounds proclaim
the burning season dies.

THE MINOR KEY

It is the minor key I crave,
full absorption in it,
view of a Spanish bay,
a single sail where cliffs
jutting out form a kind of gate,
perfect the sea and sky beyond;
the music at a Renaissance court,
idealized love turned
to pure lament on lutes
and viols, the grave walk
of figures garbed as though
statues from Roman times;
the doves in frescoes,
the eyes of supplicants,
and so much more of like intent.

To live the conflict fully,
alike for many a creature:
the lower half held back
by the weight of place
and other pulls for which
there is no obvious evidence—
underwood, desires gone wrong,
a taste for the world's rewards—
the upper parts seeking
contact with that of which
early representations tell,
the unimagined wonder,
amazement in the voice,

the thin trail of birds
rising when bodies sleep.

This mode of strain I crave,
full concert of the pain
and anguish without which
the movement upward cannot be,
pray that its minor key
possess me with the force
natural to flowing things
streaming to their source.
And not allowed
nor ready to reside in
the realm toward which all flows—
its lasting splendors and
its spaciousness—crave
that I may lament with all I own
lack of its harmony where I am.

FIRST SNOW,
BROOKLYN HARBOR

1.

Driven by a music of which their every move
in a mood of love, the loftier side of them
in dreams are parts; unconsciously out for a sign
that is a gesture of the song they do not hear:
who among those who stopped along the promenade
facing the waterfront could have regarded
the first flake of the first snow this season
as nothing but the substance that they are?

Unless someone had ventured out, had left
the customary ways of recognizing form
and light and shade; unless someone endowed
with a rare inner quality had looked
and found the single substance holding these
streaming from his eyes, breaking from the heart
where it lies and not unlike calm waters beneath
the frozen surfaces in mountain areas waits
beneath all icy grounds where light like sound
in the unsaid aspect in each song glistens
beyond sight;

       unless someone had pierced
the surfaces and stood entirely immersed
within the substance of all forms, within
the very center of all thoughts and shapes
that like the very breath of time rise from
the one sure thing toward which all strive;
unless someone in such state had given

existence to the first flake falling and from
beyond the range of sight proclaimed the whiteness
that streaked across the eye in streams
and in a time too imminent to calculate
dissolved, absolved the heaviness of the world:

who among the solitary men looking out
beyond the river and the ocean piers
into a changed and changing distance, could
have known that these are closely linked:
the forms across the waterway, the lights
barely discernible that alternate, the snow
that falls, the physical significance of snow,
the revival in the hearts of solitary men
of dreams?

How could they have known that these
are more than linked, are one with that
which glistens in and between the flakes,
are the same as what the fall of snow implies?

And what it evokes in them, how could they know
it is the same as what they—solitary men,
distances apart, gazing beyond the river,
ocean-landing where they stand—in this
first snow are looking toward, are looking at?

2.
The thing itself that lives, the dominance
of that which is so close to all it is
the heart of all; in which the first sign
originates and descends into sight as snow,
whose nature is unfathomable although

in this and every scene implied by some
incomprehensible means like a music
that cannot be heard: O what they do not know
is that the distances expand within them:
what they are looking toward is where they are.

They do not know departure is the pain they carry;
that circumstance has forced on them a burden
the removal of which is the change they seek
in dreams of a journey and the joy they sense
of what it must be like the instant of arrival.

In a fall of snow, the first of the season,
they stand and dream and watch the footprints
disappear in the will of heaven; absorb the sounds
of water-objects drown in a deeper music,
and shiver as light breaks in their hearts
and something vastly woeful hangs at their eyes.

For, if these men are in no way exceptional,
if they are not endowed with a sacred privilege
to look and find the answer contained in the question,
fire in the ultimate regions of cold, arrival
in the act of departing, the indivisible total
in each divided vanishing footfall
as each flake contains all of the snow.
If it is not for them to set forth
provoking customary habits with
a selfless motive for daring and a song
to rely on from loss to finding, they cannot know this,
though they do surely sense how enormous are
the heights that exist within the pattern of Being:

Beyond their conditioned manner of reaching, near them,
with no more than a turn of their shoulder,
they can glimpse the regions of high-minded men:
the heart which is wisdom, the pleasure, the welcome,
the compassionate quality in music.
The burden circumstance has forced on them
is a condition abolished by a shift within them,
as the heaviness of the world is abolished by
a sudden decision which is the first snow
of the season.

* * * *

　　　　　And if they cannot know themselves
possessors of the single substance
of which all of the harbor before them,
and the forms that make up the harbor
and the transformation of everything in
and around them which they attribute to snow,
are made of;

　　　　　and if they cannot assume the stand
that that which is in them, into which
each flake dissolves and all perceptions flow,
is changeless, and they the beholder of changes;—

they do, just the same, sense with longing
something of permanence, knowing, as they do,
only the changes; and for a moment absorbed
in a depth that is the quiet of the whiteness
descending, question:

what are they caught in?
Where does it come from, the dream, the thoughts
of which they are conscious? Has the snow
brought back the ways they knew as children,
dreams that have caused them embarrassment in gesture,
quick glances?

And if they cannot recognize
themselves in the radiance of unreal faces
like spirits in a net of snow; and if
what they know is not the supreme conquest
by achievement but the mystery like a sob
within them, they do, just the same, sense it:
the nearness that is far:

ranges of oceans,
distance and music in the sounds of water-objects;
and grieve for the breath of an angel they feel
in the footfall they cling to for an all-engrossing,
all-encompassing vastly beautiful moment
before the outlines that attest to the fact
that a human has been there, turn into snow.

1960

AWAKENING MYSTERY

Leaving the place to which you are accustomed,
whose unknown corners sufficiently localized
you think of less and less
and forget them day by day;
leaving the place whose mystery
is never fully explored
because it has become familiar
and you do not accept
what you will never know
that you will never know it
but forget that there is something hidden
behind your door,
something beyond the reach of lights
that you have missed, and do not know.

Leaving the place whose mystery is shrouded
because it has become familiar
and exploring the familiar is usually neglected,
it can happen one day
when you take a train out into the country,
that you find every road, every field,
every house and stream washed in a clarity,
each enriched by nothing but
its own quality:
color, shape, and angle of shade,
a horse grazing here, a bridge over there,
and something that is quick
in the distance, whose shape is lost
but whose shadow you see.

And when you pass by the brook
and behold the water in absolute stillness,
the backs of houses, a boat tied
to the bank, and you remark—
and it is only later that you know
you have remarked this—: "How still,
how perfectly still it is,
the very black shadow of trees
in the water," and directly thereafter think
of a woman weeping
because someone had made her understand,
and you are not sure if this was dreamt
or witnessed by you at some time, but know
that her experience at that moment
is something you can comprehend,

and you are moved, so moved,
to have somehow been made to possess all this.
It is then, when peace and clarity
take hold of you and you are so at ease
you do not think to think:
then it might happen that you sense
the mystery you have not explored
in the place you left,
something hidden behind doors,
something beyond
the reach of lights that you have missed.

LATE LAST NIGHT

Late last night we drove through fog:
nothing but a vague onslaught at
the window: vapors, or was it breath?

the clouds of the earth coming at us
all along the road. In the watery
substance all turned the same:

lights around corners, dreams behind
rooms, the country wide as oceans,
the singleness in every name.

IRRECONCILABLES

How to explain that on the day
we knew disease had invaded her
who had brought us into the world,
that death had conquered her like a weapon
she would not escape for long,
the winter sun spread vastly
and with utter ease
giving sharpness to each thing,
making all things stand out
as usually they don't:
a line of ships rooted like rocks,
and people in the frozen streets
free and light as the breath
that clung to them like clouds.

Along the edge of the cold sky
a strip of deep lavender ran
like a streamer in a wind
pulled by an invisible string,

and the water in the port
made over by days of cold
looked chopped but permanent, as if
the sea were chunks of bottleglass.

And everywhere surfaces
giving off the winter sun
in a sort of game of catch,
throwing at each the light
that each received, so that

the effect was a jubilation,
a juggler's feat so fast,
so intricate a trick, the full
extent of its multifarious display
escaped our eyes. But the sense
that it was there, and that
it meant not to deceive
but to reveal a joy
did not elude us.

Yet we were driving to get to her
who we feared might soon be gone.
And how were we to reconcile
exuberance with what we were about?

That a car was taking us
to the condition we call death,
that extinction could occur
when the day showed itself
in a display so bright
it seemed a game of light,
that disappearance should
make sense when all about us
objects we could not name
flared up in a cold winter sun
and shone until we had to turn
from them as from a flame,
nothing in us could reconcile,
nothing in us could explain.

ENCHANTED FLOWERS
in memory of my mother

1.

She is a flower in the wind.
Her bloom is gone.
The wind must take her petals
one by one.
She brought joys to beholders,
stinging pain to intruders.
Lean stalk of a stem,
the wind once proud of her
now wails in and about her.
The seer cannot see herself.
Dying is the wind's full grief.

2.

Flute, flute
be your utmost!
A column of thin smoke
in that forever distant distance of
perpetual light.
Thin shape by flowers
entwined as though by a snake,
the mood of dancers
collected in a heap.
Flute, flute
till I weep!

3.

In total possession of themselves,
arrayed with every pollen, petal,

drinking insect each possessed;
arrived at their own enchantment,
arrived at last in that sphere
where storms do not enter,
where not they but the winds have died:
they hum to be thus collected,
humming absorb the anguish
of those about to cross over.

4.
Flow gently, flower.
Children once again,
we weep at your going,
weep for a reception
adequate for one such as you,
absorber of light,
bearer of our misjudgment.
You who pity us when,
returned to our purity
for the instant of your going,
we cannot endure it
and you break out
in renewed petals
in the air above our heads.

5.
Contained in the air
and spread across the distance
we take in in our days,
in the deep recesses of our beings
devoted to this enchantment,
striving to experience
flood of the scent

that pursues us: flowers
of numberless clouds, of wings
of wind falling toward each stem . . .

6.
You among the rare, the chosen ones
whose inner space is wind of scent,
do not insist on the attempt
to hold the bloom in trembling hands,
nor keep yourselves from trying.
To stand straight, in the distance your eyes,
alert in sleep, in all your worldly ways
to hints and nuances that seek
the fragrance that you are:
is there any more to do
to honor flowers praising you?

7.
Who is alert is pious.
Imprints of things as they are
demolish notion and choice.
Who has the strength to replace
his will with the naturalness
of scented growth and death
touching body and eye,
glides across night and day,
is masterful, fragile as a bird:
exposed, exposed—alert!

8.
In separateness, transition's bitter mark,
an admixture of the space that gathered them
and the touch of red, of green, of violet

upon the cloudlike paleness of the frost
that curls to kill beneath each stem:
so do all move across the plain
assigned to each for our days.
What has been said is said again.
Of shadowy substance is the dance.
What's concrete is beyond such circumstance.

9.
In transition composed
the motion, pallor,
leaves of the rose.
In transition contained
the indwelling wind
that had languished once
on many a noble's parapet,
had lain within a flute,
had held upon a cheek
what to strong men is
a sign of the weak.

10.
But no! They are fools
who see and say it so.
Grandest of all,
as experience second to none,
flowers that fall from eyes
as response to
a more than human,
more than time-conditioned
circumstance.
Petals that rain
when the wind must come

to shake at a stem.
Gently, flow gently then:
flower, breathless, human.

1965

WANDLUNG

1.
Day after day, comes fall,
sky and sea are gray.
Along the coast, beneath bare boughs
there is the threat of ice.
Seasons of blossoms
and of dying leaves
have tumbled down streams
seething at the estuary
free now of summer stars
and of discoloring shades.

It is a time brisk and stark,
devoid of former flourishes.
The last of the south-going birds
have flown past
on to their separate seas.
Only the shrill warnings,
the questioning blares
of northern birds

spatter the air.
A few late leaves drift by.

2.
Down in the port
boats empty their registered cargo out
blurred in
the watery autumnal haze
as if the bales were ghosts.
Boat after boat
or so the dampened foghorns say.

3.
Yearly, when summer's ease and fervor goes
young women mostly indoors,
young men in bars
have watery, melancholy eyes
that whisper of strangers
driving their horses up
uneven streets,
foreigners who whistle like winds
and sing.

Then will even the dogs lie low
so splendid, so rare—
and yet not surprising
almost in fact anticipated
as if expected year after year—
so commanding the sight
of the bright strangers
driving their black
wet horses
up the hill.

THE DIPLOMAT

Radiant as light in glass,
it must be knowledge of home
gives his eyes the look they have
always reminiscent of pure sight
as of a child just up and in
the frame of a window looking at
meadows, trees, a country road
streaked by a spring rain.

Such confidence must mean
home is not a distant land,
is imminent, a resting place
that does not let one down,
nor is it as a wooden wharf
tired fishermen step upon,
nor as a house a boy runs toward.

He is not a naïve emissary.
Carefully he speaks and to the point,
is at ease in the world
though reticent.
A true servant at his post
he knows well what must be
guarded and defended most,
which those he comes in contact with
soon realize,
so deep the calm in his eyes.

LAMENT FOR
A GIFTED MAN

Whatever it was that gave
you radiant stillness like
a fluttering air, is gone.
You were the recipient once,
were the figure that seemed to walk
like someone wrapped in light
across an agitated bay or lake.
You could not accept
the apparition was
for our sake, not yours,
could not give yourself
to it enough to become
the radiance you were possessed of.
Now emptied of what
is so much bigger than you are,
you stumble on,
err, err,
a rower without oars,
and are off course
no matter where you are.

THE NON-HEROES

The story is not told of two young men
in ancient Greece, not friends or lovers
glorified for some heroic deed for which
they died placing gold-leaved wreaths
upon each other's brow—a fine spirit
with which their elders could identify.

These youths, and countless more,
were ardent friends because each was
possessed by a restless dream
to which they clung like erring children
in a forest to a distant gleam.
Spirited longing changed to horror
when one day each had to discover
the dream each thought the other had
was not the same, and thus betrayed—
though neither had intended it—
took to death in a scandalous way.

The dilemma abounds in modern times
though cowardice may be in evidence
where daring mattered once and pride.
A nameless yearning that pursues
the lives of wide-eyed, eager youths.
Unvoiced, with nothing earthly satisfied,
it clings to those it chooses
like a fragrance the youths attribute to
their forms. And seek the nameless,
though they have failed, in all things named.

And cannot speak of it who know not
what it is, weep to be understood,
are gentle-limbed and always lonely,
fall into bad ways and disrepute,
and cannot grasp that what must die
so they may rise are those named things
through which the nameless cannot be
achieved. And have not learned to kneel,
and are not fit for this heroic deed.

THE MIST
FROM TREE TO TREE

They seemed this morning on their way to work
not mindful of the fog they could not see,
not mindful of an eye hidden somewhere,
the sign on someone rushing by,
the mist from tree to tree.

They hurried on.
They reached their destination one by one.
The eye looked on
when they went in, when they came out.
Heading homeward on a darkening road
a fog closed in. Someone was lifted, carried.

GENTLE LAMB

At a street corner
waiting to cross: two boys.
Pressed against the chest of one
a dog slender as a greyhound,
timid as a lamb.

a tenderness before which he—
also at home in
an invisible mantle
that clings to him,

gentle as a lamb—
is himself dumb
as the animal
he carries in his arm.

TODAY'S TROUBADOURS

Troubadours in modern dress
lack luster of the hearth.
In absence of fortified tower,
glow in window toward which
young hearts aspire,
in lieu of idealized love
what are singers singing of?

The shadow of themselves
on horseback in twos,
ramshackle walls in view.
The feel of their loneliness
expressed by untamed land
and lonely, lawless place.
Immersed thus with themselves,

with their restlessness,
their stance is not romance
but awkwardness. Gone from them,
for a time at least, the song of praise
that gave many a troubadour
distinction for his lines
and splendor to his face.

THE UNWORLDLINESS
THAT HE CREATES

1.

Alien in environments he has come to for the first time,
he is nevertheless at home in the eyes of those who look
upon the strangeness he creates,

is at home on streetcorners he chances on
where men stand about discussing events of which he
knows nothing,

is at home along the boulevards where the big hotels are,

in the parks at night when the crowds have left,

in the garden where on Sunday mornings there is music
of swans,
of peasant maidens lost to madness out of love,

is at home in these as a bird is above hillsides and towns
touched on for the first time.

2.

As a face becomes real when contained in a surface that
reflects,
as the soul has an inkling of what it can be
when received in the eyes of a stranger,

what among the things that depend upon
reception by the heart
is comparable to the recognition that

the flutter of wild ducks, the cry
of wild ducks whose object of pursuit
the observer cannot trace—only the cry
pierces the park as if despair
had been sounded on a trumpet—

that such happenings one mild afternoon
in a garden of a major capital,

that the aloofness of a swan, its utter lack of agitation,

that these suggest the cold majesty, the grave
beauty of total self-concern?

That these cries, these calls, these cruel attitudes and
             gestures,

that the young man lying in the grass his face resting in
               one hand,

that the old woman sitting under a dark tree,

that both, and countless more
letting what goes on around them go by them as if
the cry of ducks, the target lost behind shadows,
the poise of the swan, and the anguish,
the reception in the stranger's heart

were no more than a slight wind touching the leaves,
no more than clouds drifting by,
no more than the mild shadow of clouds . . .

To recognize that these are no more than a slight wind
                              touching the leaves;

to recognize that to experience these,
to let them be like a final phrase—
name, place, days, years chiseled roughly in rough stone—

to let them be part of the heart's reception means

they have achieved themselves

and having achieved themselves have become less than
                                                    formless

a thing for which there is no word
for it has not the shape of nothing

and received rests there as that,
as that without change. . . .

3.
Who is he upon whom those who see him as a stranger
look as one looks upon someone who suggests a world at
once foreign and intimate, a world that though distant
reveals something one cannot quite visualize but has
yearned for, has said its name and responded with
tenderness . . .

who is he upon whom those who take him as a stranger
look and are amazed, for he recognizes himself in the
eyes of those he does not know, who all at once and for
a moment they cannot explain or even remember, know
him, and are astonished as they have been when absorbed

in the rarest of artworks, love words, songs of dreams . . .

who is he in whom the things he looks upon achieve
                                          themselves?
He in whom their forms are released and become the
essence that he is, and is theirs?

Who is he who stands before a painting in which the
mother weeps, and the father weeps, and the son has
suffered all there is to be suffered?

Who is he who stands before this painting, and weeps?

4.
Whether he stands before a canvas whereon man's
                                          ultimate
condition is expressed through the most gentle, the most
beautiful body possible,

whether he sits on a bench on a Sunday
and receives in his eyes the light
and in his arms the flesh of the candles
the women that pass him have lit
out of love for their husbands
devotion to their children and duty to parents
in the churches they have left,

and receives as well the songs they intended
the ones joined in
and the ones that shook their bodies
as they knelt or stood against a pillar
and the thought of a loved one who had come and gone
bolted through them,

and receives also the looks and songs of the men
on the day away from their routine involvement.

On the horizon the boats they will not cease to construct.

Out of the waves, out of the sky
eyes into which they can continue to look

eyes that will return to them what they had wanted to
                                                    see

eyes that will make them what they had wanted to
                                          become

the look that will give them what they had or should
                                          have had

the look that will wash away the darkness that had
                                    troubled them

will lift them to their rightful place
and make them what they are.

They bow their heads,
in the evening pick up guitars for their songs of fate.

They weep over they know not what.
                              Except that
though it may be nameless, it is closer to them
than the wind of the sea on their faces
and the light of midnight on their hair.

And infinite the shapes, the forms of tenderness

their yearning takes

The expressed of the expression is always Love
Love itself hath said

and the shapes that rise in their hearts and are dimmed
                                        in their eyes
are all as gentle, as beautiful as that body of love
that died and dies for love . . .

And receives this, the possibilities inside them,
their mostly unexpressed intention, the quality
that pours from them as though their bodies were a
                                        watery cloth
wrapped loosely around the quickest, brightest light,

as they stroll by him,
point a hand in his direction though they may be
                                        engaged in
conversation or may sit around a sidewalk table discussing
events of which he knows nothing

although at times they may look at him directly

and he is not there

only the look they seek
the eyes they know
the worship that is theirs:

the sign in the sky
the sails they construct.

5.

He in whom the pain in extremity is received and
                                      released

who is outside extremity or its pain could not be endured

he is not man, not woman,
he is not this, not that,
not I, not he, not you.

Movement transformed into art is an attempt to show
                                                this:

that form is so multifaceted it cannot be solid.
That color can only suggest color
and that color, movement and light
can only approximate
the quality the eye cannot behold,
the ear not catch,
the hand not endure.

And he who becomes he in the eyes of others,
who is alien regardless of the intimacy with which he
                                              receives
the streets he walks on for the first time,

he who is stranger to those who marvel at the foreign
                                                way
in which he moves—his ease as though gliding—

is it any wonder that when he comes into a street

when he sits on a bench or stands before a painting,

when the sky trembles in his eyes,

that he weeps?
                    For what is he but response?

And he flows into that which flows into him as a wave
                                        into the sea

and the sea into waves
and both are water
both are one.

6.

Festive the crowds the evening before a day of
celebration in the square that was once first in the city
and is now famed for its age, style, agreeable proportions,
and the equestrian statue of a king in its center.

Tomorrow, they will go to the pools, will sing on the
roads, will lie on slopes, will eat on terraces overlooking
gorges, rivers, celebrated bridges, aqueducts, historic
sites; in the evening will follow suggestions of love
through crowded streets and squares with tall fountains
whose faint spray the air carries.

They have draped flags around the balconies, there are
candles on all tables of the restaurant fenced in by
boxed hedges, and many the languages among the people
who dine; those who are local stroll in groups under the
arcades, and the places where people eat and drink
standing up are crowded.

Is it because it is nevertheless the time when separateness

comes into its own, distinct as a shadow in front or
beside one, that he turns from these, runs from waiters,
from the sounds of food being served, from drifts of
conversations?

Is it because it is the time when those to whom streets and
squares and the names of the flowers that look odd in
the night along the coast are known in a language he
cannot speak, are strangers as he is, the night before a
celebration, each alone in the darkness?

In the taxi, back to the part of the city where the hotels
                                                        are

and elsewhere and later
down the broad road that runs along the coast
he does not resist it, lets it possess him:

the demands of the night in a land that is alien—

and walks into the air to be near the fountains
and feels on his hands and face the spray that the air
                                                        carries

and elsewhere and later
takes into himself all that the light of the moon on a
                restless sea is suggestive of . . .

7.
When it is time to leave,
though he was alien where he has been,
and to those in whose language he cannot answer,

and to those who do not feel in him the possibilities in
man
and the background he reflects, is alien still:

he knows that he has been at home.

In paintings, the folds of rich garments, the dove that
hovered,
the movement of figures upward, spearlike, flamelike as a
prayer;

in the eyes of those who passed by him, sat near him,
who said much of themselves though not a word was
said:

firm glimmers, kindling suggestions of what he knows best
rose to his demands and needs as waves to stormy wind.

As if on a stool near the chair of one through whom
birds roar, flowers sway, generations sing a tale—
from whom silence rises like a sword in flames—
attentive to murmurs that follow once the word was said
(what child has not experienced this?)

he knows he will be what those around him are

who will be what he is

and that they live not only in their songs and dreams
but also in the things they make—
things that retain their human presence like a hush—

and when he leaves
                    receives their looks
their flames in paintings
not as farewell
but beckoning, acknowledging wave . . .

and where he sat and walked

wherever there were those who looked upon the
                    unworldliness that he creates

all that is air remembers him.

Madrid, Lisbon, Cascais

SHORT POEM

When eyes pass by trembling with presence,
hold on to the urge for possession of
the love without which you must learn
to remain content; then love with all you possess
that shadow wherein hovers a promise
like a young swallow in a thicket of trees.

from
A BED
BY THE SEA,
1970

UNALTERABLES

Mistakes are dredged up again,
not mine but before mine began,
of figures I never knew,
and those I did know gone,
except that since what had
been done to them is carried on
through me, they lurk about,
unwelcome presences unseen
but evident like something

moving beneath dead leaves.
I thought I was done with them.
What need had I of faceless creatures,
agitation in their hair,
uttering unalterables
in languages I refused to hear?
Other sayings filled my ears,
other directions shook me—signs
that led to gates and guards who kept

the doom-promoters out. I realized
when I returned that doom or past
were unthinkable behind those gates,
but learned that they come back,
figures of my old mistakes,
who in spite of where I have been,
what I have found and seen,
want me to dance with them
their old, disordered dance.

THE POEM

Out of continued striving
have I fashioned this.
Out of the indefinable,
its attentiveness,
yes, its embrace.

But I must add:
cold collisions—
humming, humming,
and an empty bed.

THE RELEASE

When I walk through streets
(in southern Europe mostly),
narrow, crooked streets
that look tired, worn
like old women in black shawls;
when things inanimate,
things built, things there
for human touch and presences
make me feel
that they have suffered,
that even walls, roofs, trees
bear a pain
which needs to be relieved:
the feeling that
deep sorrow resides
in everything I look at
makes me more alive.

Melancholy, sad,
but not unhappy.

What substance burns without a flame?
What human being gains in depth
who has not wept in dreams?
What moment moves us more
than when we realize
another's sorrow as our own?
Ennobling pain
must have its proper soil.

Wide, straight, new
the streets I walk through now.
Somehow I must get at what
they hide, must let their noise
go by me like the planes
too fast to spot,
must listen, listen
until I hear the silent sound
of stones I live in
as a heavy sigh.

Only in the midst of
pure suffering
will I release my cry!

DUBROVNIK

1.

What touched me about Dubrovnik
was so simple, so human:
an airline attendant going out of his way
to find me a telephone directory,
a student in his water taxi
offering me a ride as if
I were his relative,

blocks of narrow streets,
invisible presences—
pasts within pasts—
the human shadow amid these
comforting darknesses:

the harmony that stems from
relating to place and to sky,
to human need without fear
and the searching look in the eye.

2.

What makes for harmony
is engagement of dreams,
a joining with others
of the sense of
being at home with oneself,
a tie of joy
charged like a whip:

connection
at a level no one sees,
has any one word for
but each has greater intimacy with
than one's skin—
                    the dawning of
the fulfillment
always about to begin.

3.
Linked thus and dissolved
in everything surrounding me,
my limbs responded
as naturally as wave to wind.
A bee buzzed near my cheek.
The moon's thick light
dragged the sea. My touch
of your arms, of your hair
was the wave, the spray
drawn out of sight. Hand
on hand we rose from the grass.
Before us the dark, walled town.
We parted, turned once.
Between us the bridge, the sea,
streets, continents.

This town where we had met
I hardly knew but felt
its human content
as if its secrets
had rushed to my own.
I had stepped into a dream. Yours. Mine.
Water beat against the stones.

The hum of being
covering me like sleep.

4.
This flow of what we cannot name,
this depth behind the visible scenes,
this mold where we are locked in place,
that is the smile on a face in dreams,
carved smile of bliss on a wooden face:

achievement of centuries
for a town to have
access to it as one has
through a narrow passage to
a courtyard from the street—
stone benches, a fountain, some trees.

A leaf drifting on a stream.

The being
            reclining and afloat.

5.
It took time and cultivation.

When I first walked down
into the old town and found
a classical surrounding
at the edge of an azure sea—
behind the port in back of
the squares, towers and churches,
the steep slopes of

the Dalmatian coast—
the setting each summer
for a festival of music and drama,

I did not know

. . . that Dubrovnik was founded about 614 by refugees
from the Greek town of Epidaurus . . . that it became a
heavily fortified city, the center of an independent
republic, under the protection of the Byzantine emperors
. . . that it took pride in being a peaceful city . . .

. . . a city whose walls, beautiful rector's palace,
fourteenth century convents are today reminders of its
former wealth and importance . . .

   No wonder
the stones of the wall
rushed to my eyes,
the sea to my hands
as waves unto cliffs

and that love
            flourished there.

6.
Union of spirit and land.

Compounded of struggles,
of a period's decline and another's rise,
of death, first cries
when the sky breaks, and of time:

these stretches and slopes by the sea
where man is so at home
as if his surroundings
were nowhere
    but inside him—

he the drawbridge
giving passage to
a long line of figures and boats.

    ❋ ❋ ❋ ❋ ❋ ❋ ❋ ❋ ❋ ❋ ❋ ❋

Without this rush to me
of human pasts, stones, the sky,

impoverished,
impoverished am I:

without the touch on my arm
and the feel in my hand
of an accumulation of pasts
and of what is timeless
as hands move
and directions intrude.

Without these
a homeless shadow am I

when I wake
until I sleep

deprived of
environments
the sleepless presence needs.

A COURTSHIP

Intentionally or not,
I have courted loneliness.
In Spain I walked each day
from an old hermitage by the sea
to town three miles away,
refused lifts from guests,
remained by the road instead
and sighed when I saw
an old shepherd and his dog
in the fields across the way.

The yearning, the yearning
that grips me even now
when I think of sunset eyes
and the face of love
in the evening sky.

Deep in the night,
near the water in Cascais,
I hear fishermen's voices
and the chug of tiny boats.
The haze they move through
is my sleep. In the dark
a presence nears at last.
Intentionally or not
I courted loneliness
and I have met response.

The presence nearing me
is not the one I yearned for

rising from within
and covering the sky.
By now close to me
I see his flesh is flame,
his coat is stone:
to keep out the world, he says,
and hold his power in.
He is loneliness
and he is ready for me now.

But not I!
I cannot see
what waits beyond!
I cannot guess
the hardship asked of love!
I still must run
from loneliness,
must run from him
this one more time!

THE STATUE

For years I've tried to destroy
the statue in myself: baroque
facades I stood in front of
as a boy, strict rows of trees,
columns, fountains, pavilions,
sights meant for royal ease.

For harmony's sake I've tried
to rid myself of rigid
aspects. It's just as well
I don't succeed!
Someone departs, someone is wounded.
A woman runs across a street

her hands lifted in lament,
a grieving man walks from
a house with lowered head.
At moments such as these,
when pain runs through the body
and tensions flicker in a nervous sky,

the statue in a shadowed lane—
like a figure when a storm is gone—
breaks through in me, comes forth again:
and I observe with stone-
like eye, the dying
of what is meant to die.

SLEEP TOOK ME FAR

Sleep took me far, so far
a force that works for wakefulness
came to demand me back.
Caught without will, used by it
as weather does a stone or metal thing
for driving wind and snow,
I was pulled from that depth
where life's true countenance
might show itself in starkness,
instill in me its awe,
by a wind furious at my door.

And followed as I was led,
and woke because I lacked the strength
to say: "Though what in
your turbulence you hold
are worldly possibilities to which
much in me clings; though mind and will
be faded into sleep
and you have caught me unawares,
in the name of nothing less
than all the entity I am,
I say: Away!   away! . . ."

LUTENIST

That on waking
you depart from
your true home,
that the world
is not for you:
you say this when you play.
That it cannot please you,
cannot be in accord with
the harmonies in you,
what faces you in the day:
strife and disregard,
and the meetings hoped for, over—
dear shadows
merging into shadows
as you look over your shoulder
and for a brief
but long moment
look on a vanishing form.

Water in the canal
shows you windows,
panes that float,
clouds stealing away,
your face, young,
a lutenist's face,
full of dreams,
full of young sorrow.
How long, and the dark
will take the longing
hidden in the chords you play?

That the flower tossed for you
disappears beneath you,
cuts through your shirt
and falls to darkness
where you stand,
you cannot bear.

Whom, what
do they applaud
when you lift your head?
You, or their own
mute knowledge
deep in themselves?
They too have not
ease in this world,
their home like yours
is in a vault for which
they at least
have not the key!
That you, your playing
placed them there
they know when they are back,
and you—
standing before them,
bowing,
meeting their demands—
have gone away.

WORLDLINESS

Worldliness is your enemy.
Never think otherwise.
It does not tolerate for long
love that you love.
From where the pure lament
played on ancient instruments?
To what is a sob a response?
Trumpets lift our spirits up. To where?
The world is entangled with
continued decay and death.
It courts but abhors
the opposite it needs.
Entrapped in its laws
it ravages love,
hacks at truth,
weeping, weeping it must do
what is incumbent upon it to do!

How moving to think
that from time to time
a white horse does come
bringing a beautiful
redeemer in human form.

FOUR POEMS
CLOSELY RELATED

I—*Elements of Night*

Shelter was possible. Instead
we chose a sea ledge as our bed.
No conflict could be great enough
wanting to do all we could for love.
We said to the elements of night:
"The agitation at your core,
ingots of heaven thrust into
combustions to dissolve,
what causes particles to split,
the conflict causing you to seethe,
we seek in each other's arms
to burn with and appease."
Silver water foamed at our feet.
Starlight wrapped itself
around us like a haze:
the same white breath
streaming from our nakedness.

II—*Wayward Love*

Lover whom I may not see again: you
will go from my mind, not your desire.
Images which never took clear shape,
images prompted by moments in your life
when you were swept up by the marvelous
as sudden sunshine sweeps across

rough seas: all that you ever
thought of in a dreamlike way
held in your arms when you received me.
How far would you not extend them,
open them as if you could
in one impossible embrace
gather into yourself all there is!
What marks in the remembering face
it leaves: desire such as this!

III—*Lament*

There was not enough time.
The day after you took the train
I went back by way of the sky.
The night you left, the flowers on
the coast grew into my sleep
under a tossing moon.

Where have you gone? Somewhere
in the midst of a farm
where the shadow of
your weeping daughter waits
and stands like a tree at night
with lowered, sleeping arms?

We shall not meet again.
Your daughter speaks to you
when morning breaks
reminding you of rooted poles,
of limits to the land.
Too great the distance in the sky.

Who once was close turns
desperately near in air.
What should my fingers reach
but glass and clouds? The moon-
drenched flowers on the coast
now drain my thoughts.

IV—*The Austerity of the Invisible*

Beat your fists on stones!
Say the blotch on the floor
is not your shadow but your blood!
Tear yourself apart!
You did not mean to offend
but you did. You squirm, you writhe.
Are you any more than any
mean creature on the ground?
Blind screams sway in air
like bats on trees till the end of day.
The austerity of the invisible
is your experience now.
Whiteness of its mantle
receding before you
like foam of clouds or mist
withdrawing from a lake.

What is it about me
is offensive to the absolute?
Heredity? Fate?
My longing eye?

from DICHTERLIEBE

They favor him who sings of them.
He does not let them weave
garlands around his head.

He understands it is not he
they wish to praise,
it is the distances

that stream through him,
the spaces into which
they yearn to step.

He weeps when they come
with offerings,
and glides

on their expanding thoughts
linked to the heart,
certain as a man

guiding his small boat
standing up.

———————

What would they make of him
if they surprised him
on the shore

early in the day?

His deserted boat
sways some yards away.

He is on his knees
and he would seem a statue
were it not that tears

streamed down his face
without control.
What has turned

his body into stone
and freed his heart?
Who can guess

the meaning of the word
now in his head
where small white birds

have come to sit—
the word he repeats
until like a stream

it pours from him?

————————

Devoted to love, to surrender
to the incomparable expression on
another's face the instant of surrender,

he is as yet torn between
letting himself be dissolved into
the space surrounding him—

on his knees at the edge of a sea—
distance of which
his every sense partakes, taking him

to a luster behind the world's eye,
to facades that elude
the minds of architects,

to a calm
the least of tremors
can't endure . . .

————————

Now there is a portal by the sea,
and he is torn between
leaving the gate behind—

out in the distance
a man no more—
and turning to feel

the sand's heat on his naked foot,
turning to face the land once more,
to reach once more for flowers

violent atop the ridge
and vibrating in light
as if to tease the air.

It seems to him he sees in the early sun
shape after shape
of creatures of the earth

each extravagantly beautiful
entering the portal
their steps toward the land

and he sings as he turns
himself toward them,
can barely stand the throb in him

as he holds out his hand to say:
he is one of them—
and moves on toward them

perilously navigating
far out on
his tossing bloodstream.

———————

They are stunned by him at first.
His way is open and direct.
They sit in the sand moving with

the shadow of palms and the tide.
When he comes by they talk of him.
He seeks their meaning with a look across

their eyes. They shudder at this.
Is it the sky has sunk deep into them?
Their dream impossible to name?

Have they at last been recognized?

———————

He carries no instrument but
moves through the night as if
a small harp hung across his chest.

All is silent about him, and yet
it is silence he seeks. To shed
his body, his body must be

received by love. He knows
that to know his body
it must be shed, and that

to know it is to see it
dissolve in love. This is
what music tells him,

what the marks of the wave in the sand tell him,
what the scent, the breath that rises when
the body lies exhausted and fulfilled,

when there is one last beat
and that one about to give out:
what love tells him.

VARIATIONS

1.

Everything alive is sensitive.
You are off with someone else
looking at autumn leaves.
The musical key this stirs in me
comes from
helplessness, acceptance, rage—
like you, like your new love, or friend,
a body
for feelings
the inevitable conflict brings.

2.

Imagine fireworks from barges,
royal outings along the Thames,
plumes, ruffles, modes of
eighteenth-century elegance, or
other characteristics of an age.
Time intrudes. Black clouds
rifting in moonlight. A cry
no one utters, no one hears
rips the night—
conflict playing on
the dreamer as though
being
were a musical instrument.

3.

Everything alive is sensitive.
If not a phoenix, a dove,

(all right, a pigeon) lifts from
the fire of autumn leaves,
driven out of summer's death
in response to what
no one can hear or guess.
The very air vibrates
colors of fire and of fur
suggesting
something somewhere
is astir—

4.
more than my pain
caused by you
who do not mean to harm.
Needs often interact.
Not what the mind can grasp
but what is secret in us
determines what we do.
The fire has shifted far into
the sky, a single leaf
ablaze like a cry
floats toward the bank
where in the early dark—
as though
still waiting for a boat—
the human figure stands.

INHERITING
A SECRET

You have undoubtedly observed that feeling
when the scene of which you are a part—
any incident unfolding before you—
acts itself out as if directed from elsewhere,
and you are certain you understand
the meaning in each form that is part of
the whole unfolding progressing in
a sequence that could almost be predicted
as though you had read it before
in some traveler's account.

And the clarity with which you perceive
the meaning is so overwhelming
it does not last, though at the time of
understanding it seemed to you that
the state of being to which you were taken
was at once so lofty and so fixed
that then, in that very instant
all that is transient, each single part
conveyed by the form whose meaning was
revealed to you, seemed to have vanished:

as the building high above the river
and the palatial means for ascension
seem to dissolve when you behold stone blocks
and beneath the surface the dust—
and the dust a mist above the river,
and the mist depending on the strength of light
and the sound of horns for

dispersion—seem to dissolve
as do all ideas of false proportion
when a part is called and falls into place.

You have then no doubt observed that when
you stand as the ultimate beholder of parts
whose secret you inherit in a single impression,
you are amazed you did not know it all along,
for it seems so clear and certain
it could not have been any other way
and there is nothing surprising about it—
until the idea that the transient has vanished
enters, and knowledge is once again
distorted and what remains is not
the scene you beheld but your own experience.

THE WALK

Coming upon fog on the road
I stopped my walk. I tried
to blank my mind to let
the hovering dampness in.
I stretched my arms.
Thus be I hung
suspended in
damp nothingness.

Did my head fall on my chest?
My face contain that line
of blessedness behind
the necessary agony?
My palms accept the nails
of weapons, dark blood
from a barbed-wire wreath
of roses sticky on my brow?

I must have moved forward
while I hung so.
Fresh snow was on the road
and all around the road.
In tall dense pines glittered
the sun. The sun was on
the ground. A bird called.
Bird and a lasting call.

O blood! O single shrill!
Shade of the Infinite
that flows toward me

for contact with
the contours of my naked foot!
When the sun lies behind the sea
and there is even something of
a sunset for the ear,
may I thus bleed, be! and know *you*

INTO
THE HINTERLAND

Step back, step back
into the hinterland.
Palms are there, a hut
where itinerants sleep
on mats as man
passing through has done
since wandering forth began.

Into the hinterland!
You sit there on a chair
and whatever your cares may be
they stand about
impertinent as crows
waiting for anything that you
may have to throw away.

You sit there on a chair.
The rain is heavy in the palms.
The crows fly down from branches
ready to pick up
what you have gathered in
your travels and may shed
between your toes.

You throw your travels off
and sit collected in
your emptiness,
Glorious in *this* emptiness!
Everything that comes your way

may touch you,
everything that comes your way
and goes.

ALLUDING TO . . .

The realm whence comes the breeze
sustaining us in dreams—
in daily life at intervals
of thinking, musings, strain—
waits without shifting its domain
for my last, my uncompromising reach.
On earth by no other means
made manifest than this:
by man's refusal to be turned
to anything but what it is.

SOME POEMS
HITHERTO
UNCOLLECTED

THE COMPANY
OF FOUR

She dined at her usual restaurant.
Soon after she came in she found
seated near the exit door a strange
though familiar company of four.
Their looks compassionate as art
who could they be but WHERE, WHY,
HOW and WHEN in person now before her
who had so often questioned them.

Now she would ask them to explain
their own mysterious ways,
the reasons for her empty days.
And if to this they would not answer
she would beg them to affirm
her consolation: Beyond the drudgery
of daily habit, *light, light,*
our glory, would they make it clear?

Already she could hear them,
their noble answer softly spoken,
their faces a subdued holiness:
Even the raging sea is emptiness.
Grieve not. In man's extremity,
God's opportunity! But when she, in fact,
besought them, they were gone:
gone from the table near the exit door
was that exquisite company of four.

1952

NEW YORK
AUTUMN DAY,
EARLY AFTERNOON

One aspect of the scene
as I waited to cross Park Avenue
was a double line of cars
long as the eye could see
rising and falling on
the street like a gentle wave.
The other was a group of pigeons
pursuing their own aims within
the narrow confines of the street,
flying up, flying down,
in sweeping curves, in unison,
cutting streamers in the air.

What struck me about both,
long line of cars and group of birds,
was the difference in the worlds
that made the single scene.
The birds preoccupied
with their own ends implied
a stress on time and place
not only different from
that of the worm-like line
whose glass and metal glittered in
the sun, but made it seem
the special sense of speed
and time that occupied
the moving line did not exist.
And for the drivers in their cars

where were the birds, where was
their upward, graceful turn?

And then came over me this sense:
that it was all absurd,
everyone's own exclusiveness,
and that a length of time
no human mind could count
was gathered up in a single gust
of wind. And it seemed to me then
I could feel the waiting looks of men,
and it was agony to think of them
preoccupied with that
for which they have no proof.

And as the line of cars
moved on before me, I thought of
the barely scanning glance
of an indifferent, alien bird,
and of the excitement I had known
over the presence of friends
whose arrival was doubtful to the last,
who soon were missed,
and saw in my mind
the undisturbed order in the room
where these had come and gone,
and out of some increase within
which made me say it, said: "Lord,

"Lord, none of these,
not one of these persists! What is
their quick appearance but
the structure of another law?

The skyward surging birds,
the double line of cars,
the approaching figure at
the other end: these,
and every other thing
that comes in view to go,
make up no scene at all!
Their worlds are contradictory!
There is no world the same for all."

1960

IN PREPARATION OF A ROAD

They are cutting down trees
to build a road.
They are leaving acres of stumps
to be cleared away
by heavy equipment.

And those grounds with trees
not yet cut
but marked,
how desolate these
as if the trees had understood

the sounds from cutting saws,
as if the trees had thrown off
their last few leaves,
had torn off their branches
like a city besieged

and ruined by its own hand.
Disaster, it is true,
is part of the process of
construction. History is this;
and, to some extent, a

reasonable submission: to get on,
the mind imposing its will
clears what is in its way.
Rights are not questioned,
monsters fed that are best

left unattended. The drive
toward what is wanted
stirs desires
dangerous in people
in no position to pursue them.

But the upheaval
before which reason and
the past subside is this:
what is leveled, what is raised,
what is gained, and what is lost:

incidentals—
when twigs and branches
lie haphazardly about,
when motors whirr
and what is cut down, smolders.

1961

CATALONIAN
SHEPHERD

He is a cyclist now
in practice for the county race.
He has turned the care his fathers had
for living things, into a love
of noted self, of modern ways, and speed.

In the fields where the racecourse runs
a shepherd and his dog watch over flock.
Stick in hand, an older man, standing on
a rock, his presence, tall, erect
safeguards against wild impulse and attack.

He greets all passing by and gathers in
a sense the younger man is training to cast out.
The shepherd still collects within himself
a residue of feelings and of distances
the cyclist is tearing from his speeding face.

1961

SPANISH LANDSCAPE, SEASCAPE, WOMEN SINGING

1.
The color of trees
a meager, a hesitant green
due to a scarcity of rain.
Pines whose tops are like
umbrellas turned inside out

cork trees with trunks
half stripped, half sleeved
in its own pale bark.
In the full picture
from coast across hills

the trees look compliant
bereaved like the women
whose song is carried in
the slight mid-morning wind
a song to their men

to return to
their arms, half sleeved,
and the fields
turning bare—
and their men not there.

2.
Birds   some circling the bay
others perched on cliffs.

When they sit, their heads
drawn in, their wings pulled back
they look like oversized eggs.

The sky is somewhat overcast
The clouds are thin and fade
are finely ribbed and are
as widely cast across the sky
as sails of wind, or wings

Slowly they fade and change
Clouds changing into air
air turning into sails
of which somewhere behind the rocks
a woman sings   and wails.

Sa Riera, 1961

SPANISH GIRL BEGGING

She clicks her castanets
as though the furor of her life
had to be artful in her hands
or she will be beaten by
a drunken father in a Gypsy tent.

Her attraction is the power that
the outcast has: aloof, defiant,
terrifying in image and consequence
like fire or some rare
and unexpected torrent.

Dark-haired, a dirty scarf around
her head, her dress like one
a Spanish dancer wears, she has
the look of a bouquet of flowers
harshly neglected in a vase.

She alternates her beat
with ease and exquisite control
and shows her rhythms in her face,
hard and not a bit inclined
toward gratefulness.

She has no eye for those who come
to gaze upon her as a show,
and when she stretches out her hand
she does not beg, she demands.
Contrary to what most think, she knows
that begging has its rightful place.

1961

A SOLDIER WAITING HIS TURN IN A BARBER SHOP

(Cadaques, Spain)

Waiting his turn his eyes
are lost in another's gaze
the mirror holds. They had
not met before. He is a soldier.
The other came from far.

What each caught in
the other's eyes, neither can
explain. It is as if
for the first time, or once again,
they see as man sees man.

Some unconscious gleam
come up like a collect-
ively remembered land,
a peak the sea like time
has kept behind a shroud.

Walks where desires have died,
a height where, like the depth
at which their eyes now met,
thought and heart being one,
the accomplished ones go arm in arm.

Astonished, they are not yet
embarrassed but, as love is fed

by a deep memory
and fire by the things it burns,
cling on to the reflecting element.

But then, and soon, and suddenly as
the recognition came, the spell
that unified them falls from them,
and the one awaiting his turn
now has a look forlorn

as if for the first time
departed from home and cast
into an indescribable mood,
he had for the first time seen
the sea's enormous solitude.

    1961

SPIRIT-LIKE
BEFORE LIGHT

My parents are making the journey
they had hoped-for long before
the expulsion that brought us
here. Their destination
is Haifa. I went to see them off.
Their cabin was shockingly narrow.
An imposition of crude figuring.
My mother looked at first as if
this lack of regard had hurt her,
but not for long. My parents

have crossed many seas,
have been exposed
to more than one narrowness
dangerously close,
to walls too tall
too near for human need,
to bars criss-crossing overhead,
the iron web of political ends.

At such times my parents have been accustomed
to construct in their minds the doors
that lead to stairs. To see themselves
pacing up and down on decks—
sea and sky falling away before them—
attending with their hearts
the names of their children
and of their children's children
announced and repeated behind clouds.

On this perhaps the last of their journeys
my parents are once more on the way
toward the promise
their trapped and hunted fathers
and their fathers' fathers
had never doubted.

Beyond the roofs of the rooms that are narrow
the breeze that parts sea and sky
in endless succession—
for it rules there
is at home there
in whatever it is comes after the parting—
my parents have had an instinct for.

They do not need to hear the voice
thundering forth behind clouds
to know it is there
but have heeded the ancient prediction:
of Zion, the homeland, the holy dwelling.

This it is. Not a place.
It is not a place toward where they go.

They go, my parents,
whether they would admit to it or not
their whole being turned toward that—
spirit-like before light—
which no Jew will pronounce by name.

The place given as destination
is important and significant
but only in that it is the embodiment
of elsewhere—

elsewhere
where the breeze uplifts
where narrowness drifts
thin as a thin cloud
and is gone

elsewhere
where apparitions of sea and sky merging
vanish like mists in the sun

elsewhere
where the voice that is deeply embedded
in all tones
but does not speak in the world
speaks
calls home its own

calls home its own

and the children enter.

1963

SOME
NEW POEMS

THE SHIP

An Evening Elegy

1.
Small swallows chirping joyously
swirl about the town's belfries and rooftops,
fly in circles above Dubrovnik's bay
as the sun sets. Slowly, slowly
this far south, the sky's red pales,
the heat of the day subsides,
slowly the whiteness comes,
the pale time when outlines are less distinct,
stillness descends and churches ring.

A boat making a wide arc
heads for the town's small port.
From my balcony I see the boat not as
a craft ferrying summer crowds to island beaches,
bringing peasants to the markets of this town,
but as an elegant ship plying its course in a haze,
making its way across my mind
as the hours reach the day's white time.

Words repeat themselves inside my head:
Objects of yearning have made
the human being the overwhelmed
inheritor
        Soon
the long evening will start, whiteness
set in. The fiery time is done.

2.

The ship I see behind the haze
is long and white, yachtlike;
stewards bring trays, officers
are dressed in the best of uniforms.
Tapestries hang in the lounge,
the chandeliers are dimly lit.
I see myself standing toward the bow
looking out into the foggy sea.
Where have we not been, what have we not seen?
The city of my childhood falling, towers,
palaces, museums, parks and lilac gardens
swept up by the waves. The face of the woman
struggling to reach me is that of
my mother calling, but the waters
have come between us. What was
is nothing now. Even those shadows
I went in nightly pursuit of—
figures that had run from my dreams—
are drenched by the waves, their features
blurred and often repellent.
What once tempted, as though concealed in the face
were the truth of an angel, has altered
its visage. Or I have grown indifferent
and can no longer see
what once I thought I saw.

The ship has passed through the time of the fire.
Whiteness sets in and I do not think
I am ready to meet it,

do not think I am ready for
the obliterating sameness it brings.

Objects of yearning have made
the human being the overwhelmed
inheritor

3.
Where the ship comes from, or where it is going:
who has answered what many have asked?
And who could grasp the total meaning
conveyed by the look, the nod, the silence,
the words of the few who did get to
where questions are not, and became
the inspiration of civilizations and of cities?

Is it from out of these stirrings and tensions,
and because of the sacred glimpses that stand out in
the landscape of human experience like glaciers,
like monumental structures made of the whitest of rock—

is it from and because of these
that the yearning has risen,
that the ship has set forth on its way,
has passed by man's great expressions of faith and
                                        of striving:
pyramids and colonnades,
arenas of worship and theaters,
stairways, parks, palaces,
statues, fountains and hedges along waterways?

And from the walls
the silent faces of ancestors,

of kings, and of saints,
and along the walls
the gilded chairs and music racks,
the harp, the harpsichord . . .

Water falls from the ship as it goes,
water that is the ship's sole course

Objects of yearning have made
the human being the overwhelmed
inheritor

4.
And as part of the process,
part of the span the ship crosses:
I have gone and returned
and have gone again.
I have yearned and have hoped
and have reached for what
I was told I must not,
tore at the mystery like veils from the face,
took the forbidden body in my arms
and was held in turn as though by a
white flame:
for I was seared
but not burned,
whitened
as the flames in the sky died down.

And what should I reach for again
and where?
Can the day yield any more than

the sight of windows blazing,
giving off an almost blinding fire
from the water as the sun goes down?
Can I repeat what I had caught
in the shade of the alleys
when the clock struck noon, struck four
and the shutters were drawn?
The figures that stole from my rooms
while I drifted through sleep like a ship,
can they be summoned again who are gone?
And if they returned
would they have hollows for eyes,
seaweed for hair?
and their bodies the pallor of the drowned?

Objects of yearning have made
the human being the overwhelmed
inheritor

5.
All things throughout the day
are separate and distinct.
When day goes, when outlines fuse
and the past falls off,
when desires float by
like scraps from far away:
a substance that contains all these
breaks forth. Flames will come again,
but whiteness rules when they are gone.

Evening lights ablaze in windows
fade out in the sea, and our dreams mix with
the waters' even flow, but behind these

are we not as we have always been?
Is it not because of whiteness that winds burn
and our thoughts and feelings are aflame?

White, white, center of fire, white at the core!

Whiteness at the end of flights and flights of stairs!

Cloud, wool of the lamb, gaze of the animal and saint
above the heights of trees and the pillars' stone!

Objects of yearning have made
the human being the overwhelmed
inheritor

TWO POEMS
ON THE FIREBIRD

I—*Gift of the Firebird*

I will give you what you need.
Though I tremble, I am not weak.
What causes me to flutter
does not end. Free is what I am,
and you must let me free.
Who am I? The fire of my feathers,
my flaming presence only tells in part.
No one beholds all of what I am.
I may be in your eye and heart
but I am never owned.
No arms enfold me for long.
I yield so you will let me go.
Know though that my appearance here
in the shadow of golden fruit
shall not be in vain. My gift,
this fiery feather will remind you
you have held what you shall miss:
it will slay falsehoods and mists,
will free you from the grip of those
whose trickery does not live
unless you take it to be true.

II—*Addressed to the Firebird*

Ever since I held you in my arms
(a flaming presence as I knew afterward)
what is unclear and ill-intended,

the murky force that thrives on refuse,
has been dispelled. All is now in place,
pale in pure light, each rising to its
full height and worth. All I
have done has flourished into fame:
but what is order, what is gain to me
who am bound to you, my bird of fire?

As time is piled on me like frost on leaves,
wherever I go, whatever I look at
it is our meeting I relive as in a haze:
I am young, you are under a tree
of golden fruit; I have stumbled on
your garden by mistake, or so I think;
I catch you, hold you; clasped in a dance
I demand, you yield; I entreat, you elude
being both coldness of a swan
and passion of a bird aflame;
too much nearness and, my senses lost,

I let you go. Since then your gift—
this fiery feather I am left with,
your promise in my mind and heart—
has brought health where withering was,
success in skills I wanted most.
But what is order, what is gain to me
who am bound to you in no more than memory?
To have held you once should be enough,
but it is not: consumed by your flame—
a yearning beyond any worldly desire—
consuming me too slowly, too slowly,
my cruel bird of fire!

PERSPECTIVES

1.

The agitation in and on the land,
the indifferent calm of space beyond:
these two perspectives do not meet.
Both extend from man, extend from him
like roots and branches from a tree.
Each nudges him differently.
One demands his arms, his legs;
the other, of his head and heart,
makes no claim unless sought out,
is the far-off point of his return
where nothing ever moves away,
and all he wants and does
is approved of and endorsed.
Though both are his, they are opposed:
the two directions do not meet.

2.

Small birds, dark birds, birds of
the night nestling in
his hair (how shall he rest?),
whispers of a love wild as flames
lead him here, command him there:
"What have you arms and legs for?
And the milk of the male,
the power underneath your skin?
Remember this, remember this:
from now on years—
one, or ten, or more—
go quicker than before!"

Not the ageold dream nor even lust,
fright drives him out into
the nervous stillness of the moon-thick night.

3.
The indifferent space about his head,
the distances where towers rise,
gold glimmers at the end of sight,
the perspective too supreme
to attract attention to itself:
it does not beckon, does not nag him
as the one that depends upon
his arms, his legs, his skin.
And yet, pulled into
the agitation in and on the land
at night and in the day, it is
the other perspective he cannot forget,
that kinder aspect in himself
as detached from the needs
he is yet forced to meet, as are
the things that fly, from earth.

GOLD-LEAVED STILLNESS

The action that brought on my pain
I do detect but not why why I must
suffer for it, dark clouds within
that dominate my mood like a storm in
a nineteenth-century painting.
I choose the calm—indifferent though
to the turmoil (too petty?) I'm in—
of an Eastern Orthodox Church
and in front of gold-leaved icons sense
that suffering can be salvation,
that both have their roots in this:
the look of saints is fixed,
the giant cross of gold is still.

Silences sheathed in metal,
firm flames that will not bend!
What is it to them that I am anguished
(though not confused), that a storm
darkening and uncontrolled comes up,
while it lasts dominating what I feel,
see, or cannot see? Suffering is not
for them, it is for me in whom
these opposites reside: a gold-
leaved stillness I cannot submit to
nor do without; a turbulence—
mine because the look of saints is fixed—
I would not know, could not endure
but for that long, relentless stare!

HISTORY

What do we know of what is behind us?
The old town we drove through yesterday
is as remote from us now
as the century it was built,
water covering all our yesterdays equally.

What do we know of what lies ahead?
We see the old inns coming toward us,
white irregular walls, windows spaced unevenly,
women and children waiting at corners to cross.
We see the end of a town and the fields and forests
                                        beyond it,
but also hear the water waiting to cover them as we pass.

And what do we know
of what we do not see,
of what neither moves toward us
nor falls into watery wastes as we pass?

OLD COAT

Years have gone by, forty and some,
and I am suddenly aware
they have. The pangs, the feeling
that the marvelous exists somewhere,
is about to begin when I have looked in a face
and have found there submerged
one of many dreams; the feeling
that what I really am is in
the yearning most men are not conscious of—
for that horse in gilded cloth
trotting with lowered mane
toward that bright tower out of sight—
all of that, all of that is just the same.

I see an Emperor on stage.
He is dressed in the blue of skies,
a stiff glove is on one hand,
bow and arrow in the one that's bare.
Falcon, it seems to me he cries,
Falcon, you led me to my fondest wish.
Withered is all, ash my hunt
now your red wing is gone!
Falcon, my falcon, return!
Away from him I am
his language hard to discern,
the torment in his face,
the agony of his distress.
None of this has changed.
But years have gone.
I have sat in rooms

ablaze, way out, and out of sight.
I returned dragging an old coat behind,

black blotch on the floor,
painful old shadow
dark as blindness and failure,
a coat handed down, a coat
I have not the strength to throw away:
mantle that in the end is all
the gorgeously attired fighter has
to protect him in battle
and cover his death. Years
have not dissolved this ancient shield, this skin—
though it wears out in spots
I am obliged to mend, or have it done.
                    Old women
chant on   chant on
as practiced fingers sew.

RAIN, RAIN . . .

Rain, rain on leaves worn out,
washed out, about to fall;
rain as the season ends
that ended for me when I had
to come away and I returned
to where now I sit, rain
across the windows of my room
and lenses for my sight.

Two people meet, make love,
they meet again, they fall
in love, they stay together
through changes more drastic
than weather: they separate;
write; grieve, but keep
apart. I suffer now
a separation of a different sort.

I loved you, and loved
our response. Appropriate was
the setting surrounding us,
so that when we loved it was
a depth of years and years—
countless shapes that had
risen from the sea, from trees,
from dark corners of vaulted

rooms, archways, arcades—
that came to us, as we loved
invaded us, and loved again

lived again through us.
This union then of us
with those who had lived
and loved where we lay,
was love's great bliss.

So it is not only you I miss
but those in back of us
whom our love had summoned
to our bed from out of the dark.
They too are now my loss
and where they stand and wait
on old and vacant stones
is what I long for now.

LYRIC

The embodiment of what
lies at the core of dreams,
in limbs that move as in
a dance; the thrust at the heart
of eyes that pour
deep violet on one's lap,
the music that follows,
the throb at the top of the head:
what are these
but indices
to what can never be attained!
Some warriors died thus
the sun flashing in their eyes,
and others in wet sand
not able to withstand
the drag of watervoices and
the treachery in ears!

INDIA

I sit before an urn—
actually a monument
with a cavity wherein
the urn is kept.
Camphor burns, a handful
of incense-sticks.
A few men and women
stand with folded hands
and chant a sacred name.
Nearby a river flows.
Palms sway, birds call.

Though I sit before
ashes kept in a monument
in a compound with a name,
in a village with a name,
in a country, continent with
a name, I have no name for
the cavity wherein I sit
withdrawn, withdrawn—
where visibles thaw out,
rivers dry up,
and unknown winged creatures
hum, flap, shout.

ALONG THE ADRIATIC

In the midst of a town famed for
its architecture, history and location;
among its palaces, churches, Renaissance
arcades, statues to poets, to

ruling aristocrats who with shrewd
diplomacy warded off neighboring states
and kept alive a policy of selfless service
within the town's impenetrable walls:

along the walks surrounding it, among
cypresses, pines, palms, oleander in bloom
a terrible eagerness to bring this
entire scene next to my skin

comes over me, a desire

to feel the town's texture of stone
as my own, and to gather, gather
what has been, and is,
close, close to my breath!

For a generous humanity developed by
culture and history
a renewed hunger comes over me,
a greed for the life that results from this,

and I want to reach out again and to hold

in spite of many tries that failed,
the persistent dominance of wind,
the wateriness of stones and
a tested nothingness in hands.

UNNATURAL HEAT, MOOSEHEAD LAKE

Night. All is still. No wind, not a breath
of air. The lake, heavy and compliant,
lies without moving like a dog
exhausted in the heat.
The raccoons that sniff for food
when it is dark have not come out;
they lie somewhere as though drugged,
nothing but motionless heaps of fur
on the hot, the suffering earth.
No human breath but mine; and nothing stirs.

I lie naked on my bed,
the sheet thrown back,
and with the waiting night and earth
I wait. Nothing is close to me now but
my needing, my tormented flesh.
It is a moment of unnaturalness
and my long familiar tormentors—
shapes that speak of need, of lust, of emptiness—
seize the moment for their taunts
and torturing address.

They grin at me as if to say:
you thought you'd conquered us!
Conceited, you believed you'd
be unmoved as a rock,
that only angels would appear
to lift you from your deep distress
when in and around you there is

nothing but the worst of heat,
and that sick longing on your face!
Which we are! For what we are, what we are

is this! They say, grin and move toward me
out from every dark recess.
No wind is there, no air
but they who make no noise,
who do not breathe, who have
horns for crowns, hooves
for feet, they whose lust
is animal, whose perfect limbs are
of human shape, are everywhere,
everywhere their taunts, their stare.

Dead, as though dead
the lake; nothing stirs in it.
A hot moon has spilled itself into it.
Naked, I lie waiting on my naked bed.
The body's tormentors
are closing in on it.

WORDS
OF THE PILGRIM

Nothing matters to me but
inner accord.
Come, beasts,
I'll face you if I must.
I'll walk through the dark with
the unfulfilled, the lost.
Let their terror be my cry.
What is hidden
shall come forth.
Light insists
nothing shall be missed.

WESTBOUND

A call from Texas. Yes, I'll come.
To get to know the young artist
who had asked me down,
to explore what is west of here,
the east, the east having made of
my mind and heart screens whereon
roads, rivers, fields, houses are run—
scenes, figures and faces that
continue to express and to endorse
dream memories—and a cave
glimmers like the perpetual dark.

But the new, what will it hold?
Will the night-hawks circling
above pale lands glitter in
my sleep like small mechanical birds?
Will the moon on empty roads
dry and absorb my shadow
as in the scenes I miss
or will it flutter forth
in utter restlessness?

And you, who are you really?
What your compositions tell me—
of steeples sunken in mist,
your hands diving for them
as though to rescue a drowning child—
or is your ambition not to retrieve
enclosures where preludes swarm

but to get on in the world
and be known for your art?

Nothing corrupts like doubt.
But having had to protect myself
too often in a new crowd,
what now and whom was I to trust?
That every growing thing lifts up
invisible arms; that the inexpressible
embodied in man-made forms
falls from my shadow where I walk and am;
that tears in paintings, smiles on statues
are a stream that pours from me,
gladly extended from body to body—
the gift that lives on in my touch—
that I know its reality is love:
few I have met could accept or
forgive. Though some there were,
and adequate, adequate the proof.

Not for utility, the giving,
but for expression so that that
which otherwise can't be, can be.
It is not enough someone sings,
an ear must receive it, a head
sway in the distance. Benevolent shapes
shine only when allowed to enter
the sleep of the dreamer to whose bed
they have come. In exchange only,
in the giving from one to the other,
shouts the name, the name that is *one*.

What is east then, what is west?
Each a landscape breaking into
dreams, each the pilgrim's road.
This it had become when I left:
this that I needed to be reminded of;
and of my unchanged purpose
which you made evident again,
dominated by the same
as I found out in time.
We who had not known each other
saw our outlines break and merge
in the stream that held our faces,
in the comfort we felt
surrounded by appearances
that cannot be predicted:
the night, the sky
blotting out the distance
you had observed with strictness.

THE TENUOUS LINE

Listen now, listen to this:
the line you must hold on to
is tenuous, but it is all
you have to help you on.
You cannot for a moment forget
where you have been,
and what and where it is
you must clear the way
to reach.

You are not Theseus
but you too must have combat with
shapes half human and half beast.
All your desires must be faced,
and your desire for
the beautiful—to dally,
be entangled with
the deeply sensual—
leads you to this.

Unlike Ariadne I take
no girlish interest in you.
But to get to where you are going
you must defeat
what breaks out on the way.
And this you cannot do
without impersonal aid.
My voice you must learn
to listen to,

the tenuous line, to see.
The curious fact of this
your labyrinthian path is:
there is not one desire,
not one nagging call
that lingers in your dreams
that you shall miss.
What you have asked for
you shall have: triumphal

visits with cities of
the past; intercourse
on flowerbeds with
beauties of the night;
tears on sensitive faces
in response to
what you are, what you,
by saying, by a
lament, a smile, have hinted at.

You will not be denied any
of this, but this:
what you hold you will not keep.
Applause you will not assume
as yours. Like this thread
you will not be attached
to any of what
lies on your path—
unless, of course, unless . . .

Your gain will be in other ways.
Besieged, you will not shun
the hateful looks, the trumpet

blares, the outraged cries.
At dawn, you will hold
perfection on your eyes.
You will not say: "I've had
enough, have had my fill!"
but will ask to move on, move on—
until, of course, until . . .

HORIZON'S WEST

1.

Looking through more than twenty years
of work, reliving, discovering again
the passion, the pain that

went into each word, each line,
parts of my life come up,
figures that step out of the wet

dark as out of a deep fog.

I am in a wood, by a lake
that is vast and often placid
as a reflecting glass.

Stillness surrounds me.
The mountains across are the same
each morning regardless of

bad dreams or a sense of peace.
The geraniums outside my door
are damp in the early sun.

A humming bird in delicate
maneuvering gets from them what
he can. The trees are tall and lean,

full only at the top.
They suffer from an abundance of them,
from too much shade and dark.

A stillness. A stillness that
in places has a tragic look.
Sick, dead leaves have been cut down.

Silver bark lies strewn about,
the trees' broken arms and dead
pine needles covering the not

much used and much neglected ground.
A stillness, a naturalness,
much of the land nearby untamed,

a wilderness.

Going over one's work in a place
where the human touch has been
and is now sparse,

parts of my life, much of what
went into word and line,
figures that promoted them,

appear, advance toward me now,
shapes clearer than before but
disordered, diffuse as yet, as if

risen from the lake, and wet.

2.

My errors as a boy.
My brother runs to me.
He is gentle, his blond

locks falling to his neck,
his young limbs suffering,
a bird of water

chased by intruders.
He runs to me to double
his sorrow and his strength.

I turn! How could this have been?
I, much loved then and fond of
women's care and laughter,

unwittingly was with those who
pretended not to see when someone
picked up a stone. I was not mean

but preferred standards of
privilege to rebellion!
Brother, my brother!

The others. My mother, a
striking tragedienne,
a diva who would have accepted

tossed roses, the pleas
of adoration with a mixture of
gratitude and disdain.

No one distrusted worldliness more!
No one missed it more!
How you wept, how you laughed,

how you kept the world from me,
and made me desire it!
And my father, gentle, refined,

with a feeling
for pleasure. Never
a failure, never afraid of

experience, ready to go out
and see how conquerors behave
in a mostly jubilant city.

And you, my mother, weeping,
weeping, not letting him go.

These come to me now.
The friends I loved; the turned
heads, lowered eyes of those

I could not love. The women
whose care and laughter pursued me,
whose fear of what I strove to

experience, whose insistence on
demanding from me what I
did not want, made me escape them.

They clung to the earth, and I,
even then, even as a boy,
felt an allegiance as though

descended from a place I could not
name. The instinct not to be possessed
possessed me even then. I had seen

the sky exploding in a dream
and had heard voices
singing to me from afar!

I went after them, found them!
Went after them and found them!
But surrounded now by nothing but

the stillness of a near wilderness,
am I content,
am I content with

bodiless presences?

3.
At night in bed waiting for sleep
I hear the melancholy, melodious
call of the loon coming from

the lake. There is a distant reply
from I don't know whom, perhaps it is
nothing but a bird's vocal response.

The silence of nature at night
flutters about me
and to me it is the longings of

awakened, stirring creatures in
the dark, eyes that have lived
but have not lived, arms that

in spite of all they have held
hold a nothingness now:
dreadful murmurings,

the yearnings of the dead
that are contained in it.

I put my hands to my ears.
I look at the wooden boards
of the walls I am between.

A moth is busy in the light.
*Of all you have wanted, all you
have had, what of it is with*

*you now? Betrayed, I say,
betrayed and left alone by those
who meant well! And I betraying*

*those whose love, whose need
for me I could not see! I sleep
but it is as if I were being tossed,*

tossed into the air by all those whom
I wanted, and those who wanted me.
They who in life would be far apart

have come together, are murmuring something,
are saying what they are saying
in unison. I cannot hear—

Why are they tossing me,
the living, and the dead . . . ?

Too great, too thick
the silence with words
not said, with deeds

not done, with lusts
not had . . .
         Someone appears
He is short   He is clad

in white   He is there
is there   that's all   He says
nothing   Waves recede

He with them   Into
the waves   The shore returns
Huge birds fly up   White birds

4.
The blessings, my blessings.
They are all of them, all of them
my blessings. Who have cared for me,

some inadequately,
for whom I have cared, and care,
however inadequately.

It comes over me
as I drive into town:
the new day, the barely

clouded sky, the lake immense
seen from the road above,
the trees not in a grove,

the trees growing haphazardly on
a slope, the houses small,
the flowers wild, profuse:

the living, and all my dead,
my dead who are in me,
wih me now . . . my blessing . . .

At the post office, letters for me;
affections, cares, even
considerations for what,

with what strength I have, I have
attempted . . . The blessings.
The blessings, my blessings . . .

5.
The evening says: all that you see,
all that you see, is here.
It too is worthy. Uncreated,

or made to meet a demand.
All that is here is real.
It too flows into the sea, the sky

whose expanse, whose
throbbing intelligence
you will not, need not know.

All that is here goes, flows,
it is a web, a drop
upon your eye. Your eye.

The evening is its
color, a pale rose;
the lake, calm or not.

I walk up an unpaved road
and see—suddenly—
running, leaping across it

from thickets of bushes
of trees on either side—
a deer. I know

it is an instant,
an instant and it
will disappear.

I am taken beyond thoughts, beyond
words as though I had just seen
appearing and leaping before me

a god. . . . *How beautiful*
I hear myself say
when it is over . . .

how beautiful . . .

   Northern Maine, 1970